T0334328

Nonverbal Neutrality of Broadcasters Covering Crisis

Offering a critical and sensitive reflection on journalists' nonverbal behaviors during their coverage of school shootings in the U.S., this book shows how individual- and social-level factors predict broadcasters' nonverbal neutrality.

Nonverbal behaviors have the ability to transmit bias, influence audiences, and impact perceptions of journalists. Yet journalists report receiving little to no training on nonverbal communication, despite often being placed in emotional, chaotic situations that affect their ability to remain neutral during coverage. This book provides theoretical and methodological contributions, as well as applicable advice, to assist researchers', instructors', and journalists' understandings of ongoing boundary negotiations of this rarely discussed but highly impactful aspect of objectivity. Through the proposal of the Nonverbal Neutrality Theory, it outlines predictive patterns and routines that contribute to the variability of nonverbal neutrality, and equips readers, including industry professionals and journalism educators, with examples of best practice to help better plan for crisis coverage. The work draws on journalists' reflections on professional norms and conceptualizations of nonverbal neutrality, vicarious traumatization, and social- and organizational-level influences.

As one of the first to explore nonverbal neutrality, its predictive factors, and patterns across crisis events, this book provides a much-needed insight into the nonverbal behaviors of broadcast journalists at a time when the media relies ever more on visual delivery on television, digital, and social media networks.

Danielle Deavours is Assistant Professor of Broadcast Journalism at Samford University, USA. She currently serves as the 2023–2024 chair of the AEJMC Broadcast and Mobile Journalism Division. She is also 2023–2024 chair of the BEA Interactive Media and Emerging Technology Division, as well as a co-chair for the IMET student category in the BEA Festival of Media Arts.

In 2022, Deavours received the Emerging Scholar Award from the Nonverbal Communication Division of the National Communication Association. She is a former Emmy- and Murrow-award winning broadcast journalist with over a decade of experience in local television news.

Routledge Focus on Journalism Studies

For more information about this series, please visit: https://www.routledge.com/
Routledge-Focus-on-Journalism-Studies/book-series/RFJS

Nonverbal Neutrality of Broadcasters Covering Crisis

Not Just What You Say But How You Say It

Danielle Deavours

Routledge
Taylor & Francis Group

LONDON AND NEW YORK

First published 2024
by Routledge
4 Park Square, Milton Park, Abingdon, Oxon OX14 4RN

and by Routledge
605 Third Avenue, New York, NY 10158

*Routledge is an imprint of the Taylor & Francis Group, an
informa business*

© 2024 Danielle Deavours

The right of Danielle Deavours to be identified as author of
this work has been asserted in accordance with sections 77
and 78 of the Copyright, Designs and Patents Act 1988.

Trademark notice: Product or corporate names may be
trademarks or registered trademarks, and are used only for
identification and explanation without intent to infringe.

British Library Cataloguing-in-Publication Data
A catalogue record for this book is available from the British Library

ISBN: 9781032450919 (hbk)
ISBN: 9781032450902 (pbk)
ISBN: 9781003375340 (ebk)

DOI: 10.4324/9781003375340

Typeset in Times New Roman
by Deanta Global Publishing Services, Chennai, India

In all things, I dedicate my life to Christ.

To my daughter Skylar, who constantly reminds me to reach for the stars. You are my inspiration, and I pray you always know there are no limits to what you can do.

This book is in memory of my sister in Christ Sarah Singleton, who believed in me even when I didn't believe in myself.

Contents

Preface

Reflecting on my over a decade-long career in broadcast journalism, I never really considered my nonverbal communication and its potential to impact my work. Despite covering school shootings, deadly tornadoes and other severe weather events, hundreds of gruesome murders, rapes, and accidents, and countless other tragedies, I can probably count on one hand the times I truly got emotional at work.

Instead, I recall being six months pregnant with my daughter, sitting at my desk casually reading an unredacted, detailed report of an infant's rape and murder with no effect. I remember laughing with my newsroom crew after a viewer threatened to murder my entire family if I didn't stop a severe weather cut in from interrupting her soap opera. I recall feeling more stress over hitting a deadline than about being threatened with a gun while out on a shoot.

At the time I considered these encounters a normal part of the job, something that came with the territory. Breaking news events, particularly crises, were stressful but exciting times for me and my coworkers. There's a different feeling in the newsroom when a crisis strikes, an electricity in the air that sparks us into action. It was coverage of a deadly plane crash that earned me an Emmy; coverage of one of the deadliest tornadoes in history earned me a Murrow. While I was working in news, trauma wasn't negative; it was routine and often rewarding.

Yet, I can also remember the looks of horror on my non-news friends' faces when I would talk about what I'd seen that day, the sleepless nights, the "unexplained" emotional breakdowns at home. I remember the weight that lifted off of me when I finally walked away from the newsroom after my daughter was born.

It was these memories that ran through my mind years later when sitting in a master's class on nonverbal communication. How could I have lived through ten years of crisis reporting with such little emotion, both personally and professionally? What influenced me to appear so stoic and unemotional? What were the impacts of masking emotion on my personal life and my journalism? These were questions I had never considered during my time as a journalist, and they inspired me to begin investigating the individual, organizational, cultural, and social influences of nonverbal neutrality as a journalistic practice.

This book provides a glimpse of some of the answers. The research provides a starting point for journalism studies scholars to consider ways in which nonverbal communication is often ignored and forgotten, despite its ability to impact audiences. The findings suggest journalists may not be as nonverbally neutral as they want to be, and the influences on their nonverbal variability are often socialized, routine aspects of their work that are rarely thought about or challenged. This work serves as a call for researchers, practitioners, and educators to consider the impacts crises can have, not only on the individual journalist, but on their ability to serve as effective public servants and storytellers.

Acknowledgments

I want to recognize the families of the victims of these tragic events. Their pain and loss is something I cannot imagine. I pray no one will ever have to experience this same kind of heartache again.

To the journalists who covered these and other crisis events, I understand first-hand the struggles that you may be experiencing. Know it's okay to be human, cry, and feel that pain.

I would also like to thank all the colleagues, family, and friends who have helped me throughout this process. First, thank you to my editors for making this dream become a reality.

A special thanks to my doctoral advisor, Dr. Wilson Lowrey, for being one of the first people to believe in my research. Thank you for your continued guidance and dedication to this project. Thank you to other scholars who helped with this work, including Drs. Michael Bruce, Renita Coleman, Darrin Griffin, and Scott Parrott.

Thank you to Dr. Chandra Clark, who has been there as an advisor, mentor, and friend for almost two decades. I pray I can serve students with your Christ-like compassion and care.

I also want to recognize and thank my family, those given and chosen. Thank you for the sacrifices you've made and the love you give. A special thanks to Hannah ("Aunt Hani") George Wood – I couldn't have done this without you.

Thank you finally to my husband Patrick and daughter Skylar; you are my world.

1 Introduction

December 14, 2012, is a date that will forever live in my memory as a broadcast journalist. Having received some great family news on my drive in, I came in with a bit of hope ready to tackle that day's newscast. Having worked for almost six years as a local television executive producer, I loved my job and the public service it provided to our viewers.

Little did I know that just a few hours after walking into the newsroom, I would be producing wall-to-wall coverage of a school shooting in Newtown, Connecticut, watching as elementary school students were led out of their classrooms screaming and crying on live television. In the booth that day, I remember tears running down my face, struggling to keep composure as I thought of my youngest niece in her elementary school, feeling helpless as I produced more coverage of terror. I felt shame letting those tears fall, knowing a "good journalist" would be stronger than that, and I quietly wiped them away hoping my coworkers hadn't noticed. Those images haunted me for weeks, and in all honesty, they still remain seared in the back of my memory.

The shooting at Sandy Hook Elementary School, as well as countless other mass shootings and crises I covered during my news career, led to the birth of this work, which seeks to better understand how journalists who regularly witness trauma during crises can continue to remain neutral in their nonverbal displays. Through a content analysis of six of the deadliest school shootings, as well as insights from other studies, this work hopes to provide insight into the nonverbal neutrality of journalists while reporting during crises, as well as the factors that affect the variability in displays.

Routine tragedy

As a journalist, you live and trade in tragedy. As the idiom goes, "If it bleeds, it leads." Reporting on terrorism, mass shootings, natural disasters, and other everyday traumas like house fires, murders, and deadly accidents is just a part of the job description. Because when crises happen, eyes turn to the news.

A crisis is defined as "an event, which is often sudden or unexpected, that disrupts the normal operations ... and threatens the well-being of personnel, property, financial resources, and/or reputations" (Zdziarski, 2006, p. 5).

DOI: 10.4324/9781003375340-1

Media play key roles in informing the public when crises happen (Graber, 2002). Media play a major role during crisis events, potentially shaping the public's emotional reaction to the events, making it an important area of research to explore (Seeger et al., 1998). Crises are times of extreme difficulty, trouble, or danger.

The National Research Council Committee on Disasters and the Mass Media states the functions of the news media during crisis include:

> warning of predicted and impending disasters, conveying information to officials and the public, charting progress of relief and recovery, dramatizing lessons learned for future preparedness, taking part in a long-term public education, and defining the problems that led to the disaster.
>
> (Sood et al., 1987, p. 10)

Researchers show traditional media sources are a primary stakeholder for crisis information, and television specifically is an important medium for the public during crisis, due to its immediate and visual nature (Austin et al., 2014).

Journalists are used to reporting crises, and they often become routine events for journalists who face regular exposure to such events. At a certain point, most journalists become numb to the tragedy, considering it a "normal" part of their routine work (Deavours, 2022). The Dart Center suggests 80–100% of journalists witness traumatic events regularly, with 92% reporting at least four traumatic situations (Smith et al., 2019). This eyewitnessing of tragedy can happen either in person or digitally; news workers often have to watch unedited footage of these tragedies, editing out images deemed too extreme for regular viewers (Dubberley & Grant, 2017).

The impacts of the regular witnessing of trauma are still relatively underresearched in journalism. Journalists may experience vicarious traumatization, a form of post-traumatic stress response when indirectly exposed to traumatic events (Palm et al., 2004). Reports of PTSD rates range from 4–59% of journalists depending on population, but scholars generally agree continual trauma witnessing makes journalists vulnerable to mental health issues (Smith et al., 2019; Dubberley & Grant, 2017). This is compounded by the fact that many newsrooms offer little to no support for journalists who experience trauma (Deavours et al., 2022). Despite a growing interest in the ways these events affect individual journalists, few researchers explore the potential impacts on content when journalists face trauma (Belair-Gagnon et al., 2023), including how they can remain neutral in their reporting.

Professional norm of neutrality

Scholars suggest journalists have to mask their emotions during crises in order to meet the professional standards of the industry (Deavours, 2022;

Coleman & Wu, 2006). The norm of neutrality suggests journalists should not show emotion during reports, leaving such displays to sources (Schudson, 2001). As one aspect of the more encompassing objectivity norm, neutrality is enacted by the journalist having a detached and unemotional tone. As Schudson writes, "The objectivity norm guides journalists to separate facts from values and to report only the facts. Objective reporting is supposed to be cool, rather than emotional, in tone" (Schudson, 2001, p. 149). American journalism relies heavily on neutrality, the distancing of a reporter's personal beliefs and emotions from the story (Kotišová, 2019). Some scholars note objectivity broadly and neutrality more specifically are becoming less important in modern journalistic practices, especially compared to other norms like transparency (Kotišová, 2019; Weinberger, 2009). Yet, interviews with professional journalists in print, digital, and broadcast mediums suggest neutrality is still one of the essential professional boundaries, helping define what "good journalism" is and how journalists should report (Deavours, 2022).

Prior research suggests neutrality of news coverage is socially constructed, an aspect of the professional routine of objectivity that has been referred to as a *guiding principle often religiously practiced*; as a *standard of excellence* for "good journalism"; as an *agent of legitimization* for the profession and industry of journalism; and as a *strategic ritual* for individual journalists to follow in order to work efficiently (Schudson, 2001; Tuchman, 1972, 1978). The professional norm of neutrality is negotiable and negotiated within journalism, and there are various levels of influence on adherence to or deviation from neutrality norms (Shoemaker & Reese, 2014). As a typification and routine of journalistic work, neutrality may vary and change, depending on influences by and within various social contexts.

Nonverbal neutrality norms

While the neutrality norm of American journalism has a rich history of study, it is typically explored in the context of written or verbal communication. This book builds on current understandings of the norm by applying nonverbal theories to the negotiations of the *nonverbal neutrality* of journalists during crises.

Nonverbal communication, which refers to any form of information sharing that is not done through written or spoken words, is an important aspect of all human communication. Nonverbal behavior can transmit the potential bias of the journalist to audiences; influence audience perceptions of the journalists and the events being covered; and affect audience attitudes, beliefs, and actions (i.e. Banning & Coleman, 2009; Miller et al., 2010). Because of these potential effects, the patterns built by journalists' neutrality choices, and the ubiquity of nonverbal behavior, the nonverbal neutrality of journalists should be further explored to increase understanding of normative behaviors during crisis coverage and how this comes about.

While prior literature in news sociology has examined ways neutrality has been constructed and its various contexts, journalists' nonverbal neutrality and the factors that shape it are understudied. Two common approaches to studying nonverbal communication suggest possible directions for research on factors shaping nonverbal neutrality in news.

Nonverbal theories: BET and BECV

According to Ekman's Basic Emotions Theory (BET), nonverbal behavior can reflect a biological response to internal emotions, and those responses tend to be universal, although they are thought to be somewhat controlled in the presence of cultural or social influences (Ekman, 1984, 1999). However, Fridlund's (2002, 2017) Behavioral Ecology View of Facial Displays (BECV) suggests nonverbal expression can be more of a cultural and relational phenomenon, reflecting the perceived appropriateness of behavior (e.g. social norms and expectations) in social situations as a transactional behavior rather than an uncontrollable one. BECV suggests people behave nonverbally, whether consciously or unconsciously, to achieve specific goals in interaction, suggesting nonverbal behavior is more strongly influenced at the social level (Patterson, 2019). From these two theoretical frameworks, BET provides a basis for examining individual-level, psychological response influences on the nonverbal behavior of journalists, while BECV suggests examining influences from social-level typification factors on the ways journalists control and construct nonverbal frames in their reports. BET and BECV suggest nonverbal communication is shaped by both individual-level emotional response as well as social-level factors, and so these approaches orient this book's investigation of possible influences on neutral nonverbal communication.

Individual-level factors: BET

By examining factors that could potentially change the *psychological*, emotionally reactive state of individual journalists during a crisis, the research can help explain influences that operate on the individual level and how they affect nonverbal neutrality during crisis, reflecting a BET approach. Examples of factors that could influence this emotional, reaction-based nonverbal variability include those that make the shooting event seem more severe (such as the age of victims or the number of people killed), the proximity to the event (whether in physical location, emotional connection to the affected community, or chronemic (time) closeness to the start of the event), and demographic factors like a broadcaster's gender and race. These factors change the individual-level perception of the stimuli or the trauma and, thus, potentially create differences across reactions to those stimuli.

Because BET also suggests nonverbal communication is an emotion-based reaction, rather than a utilitarian form of interaction with others, this research will measure nonverbal reaction in broadcasters as emotionally valenced (positive, negative, or neutral) reactions. A Janis–Fadner (*JF*) coefficient (discussed in more detail in the methods section), which is sensitive to emotional valence, is used as one measure of journalists' nonverbal behavior.

Typification-level factors: BECV

In addition, the research examines *typifications* of journalistic work as social-level influences on nonverbal behaviors through the lens of BECV. Thus, the work will explore boundary negotiations of professional nonverbal neutrality norms. Typifications of journalistic work are ways that journalists "mentally rehearse and build a story template" for various situations, even nonroutine events or crises – socially shared categories that serve as shortcuts for journalists to make news practices more familiar and less uncertain as they face an uncertain world (Berkowitz, 1992, p. 45). Typifications have been shown to be important factors in channeling journalists' decision-making about news and in the development of work routines (Berkowtiz, 1992; Tuchman, 1972). The coverage of crisis events, which are highly uncertain, tends to bring very high ratings for television news, making them profitable for news organizations and making it more likely that organizational factors shape journalists' coverage (Althaus, 2002). Therefore, newsrooms are often willing to shift a lot of resources, including personnel, equipment, and time, in order to continuously cover the event for days and even weeks (Sylvie & Gade, 2015). Social-level predictive factors are conceptualized as socially agreed-upon categories of how to accomplish work or "social typifications," as BECV suggests nonverbal behaviors are tools to meet standards and goals of social interactions (McKinney, 1969). Typifications in this study include journalistic role performances, news frames, news topics, and news sources – all conceptualized as socially agreed-upon categories that help to organize, routinize, and channel journalistic work.

Because BECV theorizes nonverbal communication as a functional tool, rather than an emotional reaction to stimuli, the research will also measure nonverbal behavior as strict muscle movements that are either positioned in the neutral or nonneutral plane through the measure of the nonverbal neutrality score (*NNS*) (discussed in more detail in the methods section).

By exploring both the relative neutrality of muscle movements that compose nonverbal communication, as well as the emotionally valenced reactions to stimuli, it is hoped that this research will contribute to a greater understanding of both nonverbal theories, as well as methodological nuances of studying nonverbal neutrality in journalism. The research will utilize the context of crisis journalism, specifically using school shootings as its case study for examining nonverbal behavior and its influences.

Nonverbal neutrality during crisis events

For journalists, crisis coverage is a specific kind of journalism that relies on navigating uncertain situations that are often professionally and personally challenging. It is helpful to study crisis journalism because the values of the field, including objectivity, neutrality, and impartiality, are constantly challenged during crises (Olsson & Nord, 2015). Previous studies have found that the coverage of a crisis event is more emotional in television reports than print, even when considering only language as opposed to visuals (Cho et al., 2003). Journalists who are reporting during crises are faced with ongoing dilemmas over the need to remain neutral, detached, and unemotional, while simultaneously surrounded by trauma, suffering communities, victims and their families, and death. Previous studies find journalists often feel like they have little to no training for these situations, leaving them without professional guidance on how to act (Deavours, 2022).

Covering these events can impact journalists on a psychological, emotional level, which can affect a broadcaster's ability to control or conceal non-neutral behavior. Trauma research suggests journalists working on the scene of a crisis can experience vicarious traumatization, the countertransference of empathy and trauma as a crisis worker witnesses the traumatic experiences of others (Palm et al., 2004). Psychologists have reported vicarious traumatization forces crisis workers to rigidly follow rational routines initially, but as the event continues, overwhelming emotions and compassion fatigue cause breakdowns in professional performance and quality of work (Phipps & Bryne, 2003; Collins & Long, 2003). Journalism researchers suggest vicarious traumatization leads to less adherence to neutrality norms during a crisis with overwhelming emotions and nonneutral nonverbal behaviors occurring during news reports (Coleman & Wu, 2006; Graber, 2002).

Yet, vicarious traumatization and subsequent emotional response are not necessarily experienced by every journalist; many journalists claim to be able to work deadly scenes with little to no impact on their emotional capabilities (Seely, 2019; Deavours, 2022). In addition, trauma theory suggests crisis workers will not experience the same level of vicarious traumatization throughout the event, with it being easier to control reactions in some situations than others (Pyevich et al., 2003; Phipps & Bryne, 2003). Because not everyone experiences vicarious traumatization and not everyone experiences it at the same levels, journalists' emotional response could contribute to the individual-level variability of nonverbal behavior during crisis coverage.

Crises can also show the interplay between these individual and social influences on the adherence to or deviation from neutrality norms. While typically newsrooms set policies that reporters are required to follow, crises call for greater autonomy in individual journalists' decision-making, given the uncertainty and developing nature of the events (Graber, 2002). This research will explore the potential impacts of both individual-level and social-level influences on journalistic work during crises, examining the interplay of journalists' emotional reactions to traumatic stimuli with their negotiation of the typified expectations of journalistic work.

Conclusion

The researcher hopes that, by bridging gaps in existing literature on the norm of neutrality with nonverbal communication theories, the negotiations of meaning of nonverbal neutrality in journalism can be more clearly understood. In addition, results should shed additional light on the theory of crisis coverage (Graber, 2002), which predicts how journalists work to maintain neutrality during crises. In summary, these findings can potentially extend current theoretical understandings of crisis coverage patterns, routines, and roles, as well as the psychological reactions of professional journalists, by adding crisis journalism as a new context for nonverbal theory.

References

Althaus, S. L. (2002). American news consumption during times of national crisis. *PS: Political Science & Politics, 35*(3), 517–521.

Austin, L., Liu, B. F., & Jin, Y. (2014). Examining signs of recovery: How senior crisis communicators define organizational crisis recovery. *Public Relations Review, 40*, 844–846.

Banning, S., & Coleman, R. (2009). Louder than words: A content analysis of presidential candidates' televised nonverbal communication. *Visual Communication Quarterly, 16*(1), 4–17.

Belair-Gagnon, V., Holton, A. E., Deuze, M., & Mellado, C. (2023, forthcoming). *Happiness in journalism*. Routledge.

Berkowitz, D. (1992). Routine newswork and the what-a-story: A case study of organizational adaptation. *Journal of Broadcasting & Electronic Media, 36*(1), 45–61.

Cho, J., Boyle, M. P., Keum, H., Shevy, M. D., McLeod, D. M., Shah, D. V., & Pan, Z. (2003). Media, terrorism, and emotionality: Emotional differences in media content and public reactions to the September 11th terrorist attacks. *Journal of Broadcasting & Electronic Media, 47*(3), 309–327.

Coleman, R., & Wu, D. (2006, June 7). More than words alone: Incorporating broadcasters' nonverbal communication into the stages of crisis coverage theory –evidence from September 11. *Journal of Broadcasting & Electronic Media, 50*(1), 1–17.

Collins, S., & Long, A. (2003). Too tired to care? The psychological effects of working with trauma. *Journal of Psychiatric & Mental Health Nursing, 10*, 17–27.

Deavours, D. (2022). Nonverbal neutrality norm: How experiencing trauma affects journalists' willingness to display emotion. *Journal of Broadcast and Electronic Media, 67*(1), 112–134.

Dubberley, S., & Grant, M. (2017). Journalism and vicarious trauma: A guide for journalists, editors and news organisations. First Draft. https://firstdraftnews.org/wp-content/uploads/2017/04/vicarioustrauma.pdf

Ekman, P. (1984). Expression and the nature of emotion. In K. Scherer & P. Ekman (Eds.), *Approaches to emotion* (pp. 319–344). Erbaum.

Ekman, P. (1999). Basic emotions. In T. Dalgleish & M. Power (Eds.), *Handbook of cognition and emotion* (pp. 45–60). John Wiley & Sons Ltd.

Fridlund, A. J. (2002). The behavioral ecology view of smiling and other facial expressions. In M. H. Abel (Ed.), *Mellen studies in psychology, Vol. 4. An empirical reflection on the smile* (pp. 45–82). Edwin Mellen Press.

Fridlund, A. J. (2017). The behavioral ecology view of facial displays, 25 years later. In J.-M. Fernández-Dols & J. A. Russell (Eds.), *Oxford series in social cognition and social neuroscience. The science of facial expression* (pp. 77–92). New York, NY: Oxford University Press.

Graber, D. (2002). *Mass media and American politics* (6th ed.). CQ Press.

Kotišová, J. (2019). An introduction to crisis reporting: Setting out. In *Crisis reporters, emotions, and technology* (pp. 1–28). Palgrave Macmillan, Cham.

McKinney, J. C. (1969). Typifications, typologies, and sociological theory. *Social Forces, 48*(1), 1–12.

Miller, A., Coleman, R., & Granberg, D. (2010). TV anchors, elections & bias: A longitudinal study of the facial expressions of Brokaw, Rather, Jennings. *Visual Communication Quarterly, 14*(4), 244–257.

Olsson, E. K., & Nord, L. W. (2015). Paving the way for crisis exploitation: The role of journalistic styles and standards. *Journalism, 16*(3), 341–358.

Palm, K. M., Polusny, M. A., & Follette, V. M. (2004). Vicarious traumatization: Potential hazards and interventions for disaster and trauma workers. *Prehospital and Disaster Medicine, 19*(1), 73–78.

Patterson, M. L. (2019). A systems model of dyadic nonverbal interaction. *Journal of Nonverbal Behavior, 43*, 111–132.

Phipps, A., & Byrne, M. (2003). Brief interventions for secondary trauma: Review and recommendations. *Stress and Health, 19*, 139–147.

Pyevich, C., Newman, E., & Daleiden, E. (2003). The relationship among cognitive schemas, job-related traumatic exposure, and posttraumatic stress disorder in journalists. *Journal of Traumatic Stress, 16*, 325–328.

Schudson, M. (2001). The objectivity norm in American journalism. *Journalism, 2*(2), 149–170.

Seeger, M. W., Sellnow, T. L., & Ulmer, R. R. (1998). Communication, organization, and crisis. *Communication Yearbook, 21*, 231–275.

Seely, N. (2019) Journalists and mental health: The psychological toll of covering everyday trauma. *Newspaper Research Journal, 40*(2), 239–259.

Shoemaker, P., & Reese, S. (2014). *Mediating the message in the 21st century: A media sociology perspective*. Routledge.

Smith, R., Newman, E., Drevo, S., & Slaughter, A. (2019). Covering trauma: Impact on journalists. Dart Center for Journalism and Trauma. https://dartcenter.org/content/covering-trauma-impact-on-journalists

Sood, R., Stockdale, G., & Rogers, E. (1987). How the news media operate in natural disasters. *Journal of Communication, 37*(3), 27–41.

Sylvie, G., & Gade, P. (2015). Changes in news work: Implications for newsroom managers. *Journal of Media Business Studies, 6*(1), 113–148.

Tuchman, G. (1972). Objectivity as strategic ritual: An examination of newsmen's notions of objectivity. *American Journal of Sociology, 77*(4), 660–679.

Tuchman, G. (1978). *Making news: A study in the construction of reality*. New York: Free Press.

Weinberger, D. (2009, August 28). Transparency: The new objectivity. KM World. https://www.kmworld.com/Articles/Column/David-Weinberger/Transparency-the -new-objectivity-55785.aspx.

Zdziarski, E. L. (2006). Crisis in the context of higher education. In K. S. Harper, B. G. Paterson, & E. L. Zdziarski (Eds.), *Crisis management: Responding from the heart.* National Association of Student Personnel Administrators.

2 Nonverbal theories

BET/BECV

This chapter begins by defining nonverbal communication and two primary theories about nonverbal communication, Basic Emotions Theory (BET) and the Behavioral Ecology View of Facial Displays (BECV). These two approaches provide a rationale for exploring the nonverbal behavior of journalists at both an individual and social level. This work provides a bridge between the nonverbal communication field and journalism studies, allowing future scholars to build upon the foundation and continue studying nonverbal communication in media contexts with shared concepts and definitions.

Nonverbal communication defined

Nonverbal communication is defined as a process of transmitting and receiving information without using words (Welch, 2019). Matsumoto et al. (2012) defines "nonverbal communication as the transfer and exchange of messages in any and all modalities that do not involve words." Communication is a process of information sharing and when done so beyond words is nonverbal communication.

Nonverbal behaviors are defined as actions that are performed and serve particular functions within nonverbal communication. Hall and Knapp (2013) identify "all potentially informative behaviors that are not purely linguistic in content" as nonverbal behaviors.

An example of a nonverbal behavior is a smile, the upturning of muscles around the mouth in a particular way. The behavior is the action that leads to the transmission of information; however, the behavior alone can't communicate as there is a reliance on the process of encoding and decoding by senders and receivers. Therefore, nonverbal behaviors or displays can only have significant influence when there is shared meaning through the process of communication.

The nonverbal communication field is made up of types as well. The definitions of these boundaries aren't always clear, but often include kinesics (communication through movement), vocalics (vocal range, volume, tone, speed, etc.), haptics (touch), proxemics (space or place), artifacts and environment (objects, clothing, adornments), olfactics (smell), and chronemics

DOI: 10.4324/9781003375340-2

(time) (Reitzel et al., 2023). This work focuses primarily on kinesics as it is one of the strongest cues in communicating information, and kinesics is also dependent on cultural display rules, intrinsically held within norms and standards of behavior for a group or region (Matsumoto, 2006), which is important for understanding journalistic and professional norms of nonverbal behavior.

Within these areas of study, there are even further divisions. For instance within kinesics is the study of facial expressions (muscle movements in the face that express information), oculesics (eye contact), gestures (body movements not on the face), emblems (gestures corresponding to a word), illustrators (gestures that emphasize ideas), affect displays (feeling or emotional movements), regulators (gestures that move the flow of conversation), and more.

It is important to note facial expressions are not synonymous with emotions, as you can move muscles without having internal feelings. These kinds of distinctions are critical to the study of nonverbal communication, as the breadth of the field is wide; scholars wishing to explore nonverbal communication in media contexts should find which area of the discipline to situate their study in and have shared meaning and definitions of specific types of nonverbal communication.

Importance of studying nonverbal communication

My first nonverbal communication professor told me, "You cannot not communicate." This statement has long stuck with me as a nonverbal scholar, as it suggests the pervasiveness of nonverbal communication in our everyday lives. Nonverbal communication is always present.

Within the process of nonverbal communication, we share information through various types of actions and cues, and as a group or culture, we assign meanings to these behaviors to interpret what the speaker is communicating. These often become socially learned behaviors, enacted subconsciously without thinking (Reitzel et al., 2023).

For instance, in many Western cultures, a person doesn't have to think about smiling when they meet someone new for the first time; they've done it so often they know it's the culturally appropriate greeting. Someone in an East Asia community may greet someone autonomically with a bow, as that's what they've learned is culturally appropriate. These examples show the large influence of culture on nonverbal communication (Birdwhistell, 1970; Matsumoto, 2006).

Nonverbal scholars suggest as much as 65–85% of information is transmitted through nonverbal cues (Matsumoto et al., 2012). Yet, it is often paired with verbal communication, serving different functions in the overall message (Wrench et al., 2020). Functions include:

- emphasis, such as saying "I'm sorry" while looking down and taking a low, serious tone

- contradicting, such as saying "I'm sorry" but having angry affect displays and a flippant vocal tone
- accenting a particular word or message part, such as gesturing outwardly on the "sorry" of an apology
- repeating behaviors where linguistic and nonverbal meanings are equal, such as nodding your head when saying "yes"
- regulating conversation flow, such as nodding while others speak to encourage conversation
- substituting behaviors that replace verbals, such as giving a thumbs up to mean "good"

These primary functions of nonverbal communication serve important roles in the overall information sharing process.

Studies also suggest communicators display unconscious bias in nonverbal behaviors (Ross, 2008) – sharing meanings they may not intend to share. This is common in studies of microaggressions (Matsumoto, 2006). Nonverbal communication can influence audiences' perceptions of the speaker, as well as the audience's attitudes, beliefs, and future actions about the communication event (i.e. Burgoon et al., 1990). Thus, studying nonverbal behaviors is important to understanding how information is shared.

Dominant nonverbal theories: BET and BECV

Conceptualizing nonverbal communication can be challenging, as scholars approach nonverbal cues differently. Some nonverbal scholars focus on nonverbal behaviors as indicators of biological, psychological, or emotional reactions to stimuli (Ekman & Friesen, 1976; Cohen et al., 2007). Others have focus on the functions of those behaviors, the ways behaviors can communicate information through a transmission process. A distinction between (a) nonverbal behavior as automatic and universal and (b) nonverbal behavior as functional and relational is important as scholars must consider that behaviors can serve multiple functions depending on social context, and are not always displayed in similar ways for the same purposes.

This text examines nonverbal communication from both perspectives, adding to the current media studies literature. Two dominant nonverbal theories are described below.

Basic Emotions Theory

Paul Ekman's development of the neurocultural theory of emotions (or BET) has been a prominent part of nonverbal communication research. Ekman's (1984, 1999) BET relies on the assumption of the universality of emotions, that there are prototypical expressions that are unconscious displays of internal states.

BET relies on a paradigm of evolutionary and biologic responses to stimuli, and draws from work by Charles Darwin that nonverbal expression was movement of the body that displayed internal states (Crivelli & Fridlund, 2019). For example, through a BET lens, a smile during a first meeting between people would be a reflection of the person's internal state of happiness or hope for that relationship. Scholars adopted this belief that nonverbal behaviors were external displays of internal feelings to support the idea that nonverbal displays were automatic and difficult to control, which was universal across humans (Ekman, 1984, 1999). Ekman further developed this idea with his research on cross-cultural facial expressions, finding there were six prototypic, universal expressions that were produced by basic emotions. This was the underpinning idea of BET, that facial expressions are reactions to stimuli and produced in identical ways by everyone (Ekman, 1984, 1999).

However, Ekman and other nonverbal scholars recognized that these basic emotions were not displayed in the exact same ways by every individual all the time. Ekman suggested that there could be "blended" expressions, where a person does not display in the prototypic way all the time because they are having conflicting emotions or transitioning from one emotion to another (Ekman & Friesen, 1972). This means a speaker could simultaneously show positively and negatively valenced facial movements to create a blended expression.

Ekman and Friesen (1976) also found microexpressions, or ways of masking or altering the prototypic expressions. They suggested these were often controlled by display rules, ways that culture affects the presentation of those prototypic expressions. For instance, if a person is experiencing an extreme negative state in a situation that, culturally, calls for a more neutral display, they would purposefully alter their display in order to adapt to the expectations of the surrounding culture. Culture is important in nonverbal communication display rules because it helps individuals determine appropriate nonverbal displays, depending on contexts and situations (Matsumoto, 2006), and may influence the individual's desire to conceal their nonverbal reaction during inappropriate situations.

Additionally, they suggest there are times in which the speaker is unable to control their nonverbal behaviors, meaning those behaviors will begin to be evident despite a communicator's best efforts to conceal them – what is called "emotional leakage" by nonverbal scholars (Ekman & Friesen, 1969). This emotional leakage produces unwanted displays, and Ekman and Friesen suggested it was caused by being exposed to highly emotional stimuli that left the communicator psychologically and biologically unable to conceal nonverbal behaviors.

Applied to broadcasters, BET would suggest all journalists would likely display similarly during a crisis based on reactions to the traumatic, emotional stimuli of the event. Their reactions would be emotional reflections of their internal states, positive, negative, or neutral responses to what was going on around them. This is more of an individual-level approach, less impacted by cultural or social influences, even though BET has grown to accept some level of influence on these prototypic expressions from cultural or social expectations. Despite BET's continued use, many scholars have criticized certain inconsistencies in its premises and worked to find alternative ways of conceptualizing displays.

Critiques of Basic Emotions Theory

Through his work in BET, nonverbal scholar Alan Fridlund (2002, 2017) claims to have found irreconcilable inconsistencies in its theoretical premises. First, Fridlund believed that the use of photo-matching techniques in Ekman's experiments across cultures led to a circular logic, where participants were given limited options and limited images that forced a perception of universality. Second, some nonverbal scholars suggest there are large differences among BET scholars about what should be defined as universal emotions, with even Ekman and Friesen using different terms within their own studies, sometimes having six displays and sometimes seven (Crivelli & Fridlund, 2019). As the theory continued to be used, scholars would also claim to "find" new prototypic emotions from self-reports with very little proof of their universality (Crivelli & Fridlund, 2019). Third, Fridlund (2002, 2017) and others argue that when the prototypic emotions were not found in experiments, Ekman and Friesen (1976) adapted BET to allow for cultural display rules, which supported more of an evolutionary perspective than the original biologic, universal premise. This was further intensified when Ekman and Friesen claimed these cultural display rules could be so pervasive that people would alter their prototypic emotions even in private; this meant that there could never be a way to support whether a display was the prototypic one because every expression could potentially be adapted for cultural influences (Crivelli & Fridlund, 2019). This would mean BET researchers had no way of knowing what was and was not an "authentic," prototypic expression. These critiques of BET have led to many calling the theory outdated and too narrow in its focus (Crivelli & Fridlund, 2019). With one of the dominant theories in the field under critique, another theory was constructed to conceptualize nonverbal behavior.

Behavioral Ecology View of Facial Displays

BECV was developed in the 1990s by Fridlund after his work with BET scholars like Ekman, Friesen, and Izard. Fridlund (2002, 2017) proposed BECV, which conceptualizes nonverbal behavior as a social tool that provides flexible ways of evolving displays to interact with others for personal benefit. BECV abandons BET's premise that expressions were universal or emotions-based, using a more functionalist and external approach. BECV suggests displays depend solely on interactions and contexts of the social world. Nonverbal behaviors are not truly expressions of anything in particular; they hold no intrinsic meaning and are not reliant on internal states. Instead, they are ritualized via natural selection processes, or they can be social conventions of behaviors that reward or harm the communicator in relationships.

Scholars also suggest that the speaker's nonverbal behavior is really a tool used to meet a goal or expectation, regardless of whether the nonverbal behavior is conscious or unconscious (Patterson, 2019). Some nonverbal behaviors become so deeply ingrained in societal expectations that they can be determined as the best tool for that circumstance, even without conscious thought (Fridlund, 2002, 2017).

For example, a person may smile at someone in a first meeting to encourage a friendly rather than adversarial relationship without ever thinking about the gains of smiling specifically; smiling is what has evolved as the appropriate behavior over time, a self-presentation tool used as far back as early humans (Fridlund, 2002, 2017).

Over time, these nonverbal behaviors used as tools were ritualized and routinized for particular situations (Fridlund, 2017), allowing the behavior to become almost immediate in recurring circumstances, regardless of whether the person is truly happy to meet the person or not. Instead of relying on experiments or self-reports, BECV scholars tend to use observational patterns from real-world interactions in order to get reliable contexts and social interactions through which to study. BECV scholars also study behavior appropriateness.

When applied to broadcast journalists a BECV-informed measure of nonverbal expression would be appropriate for examining whether nonverbal facial movement adheres to or deviates from a professionally acceptable standard of neutrality. The presence or absence of movement of expressions would be the focus rather than emotional valence.

While BECV does not allow for categories of emotions like BET does, some scholars suggest it is a better framework for interpreting the complexities of nonverbal displays. BECV scholars have also been able to adapt their work for non-human technologies, leading to advancements in mediated contexts as well (Fridlund, 2017). Through its critique of the original BET, BECV has become another way to study nonverbal communication and expressions through a sociology of expression. Together, the theories of BET and BECV suggest that both individual- and social-level factors of influence on nonverbal behavior may be explored.

Measuring BET and BECV conceptualizations for nonverbal neutrality

Thus, nonverbal scholars conceptualize nonverbal behavior in two ways: as reactions to stimuli that reflect internal emotional states, which is based in BET assumptions; or as functionalist movements of muscles to adhere to cultural expectations in order to reach a personal goal within a social interaction, which is based in BECV assumptions. Because of these differences in the conceptualization of nonverbal expressions, this study utilizes two measures of nonverbal behavior through which to examine the variability of nonverbal neutrality in broadcasters. The two measures are explained in detail in the methods section, but they are broadly outlined here to help shed light on the different conceptualizations of nonverbal neutrality.

The first measure of nonverbal neutrality is the "nonverbal neutrality score" or *NNS*. This measure reflects the movement of the nonverbal expression, rather than the valence of that expression. Knapp and Hall (2002) define the six nonverbal dimensions according to positive, negative, and neutral movements of muscles in each of these six areas, but the positive and negative definitions do not correspond directly to favorable or unfavorable, where a journalist is necessarily showing positive or negative emotions. Instead, they denote the direction of the muscular movement away from the neutral state, which is culturally shaped and socially constructed. The measure does not distinguish between the movements as positive or negative, emotionally. Therefore, the *NNS* is a measure of an accumulation of neutral and nonneutral expressions across the six nonverbal dimensions. The higher the *NNS*, the less neutral the presentation is overall, while the lower the *NNS*, the more neutral the presentation is. This measure reflects the theoretical bases of BECV since it examines the adherence to or deviation from neutrality as a practice that adheres to professional journalism norms. It's measuring nonverbal expression.

The second measure reflects the valence of nonverbal reaction. The Janis–Fadner coefficient of imbalance (*JF*) measures the relative proportion of positive (favorable) to negative (unfavorable) expressions, while controlling for the overall number of expressions. Each expression among the six nonverbal dimensions is given equal weight in the measure. It also eliminates the problem of having positive and negative values canceling each other out when the six dimensions are combined. Thus, *JF* is the extent of difference in the ratio of positive, negative, or neutral expressions in the broadcaster's presentation. The more positive the *JF* is, the more favorable or emotionally positive the nonverbal reaction is during the presentation, such as displaying emotions of joy, surprise, or contentment; the more negative the *JF*, the more unfavorable or emotionally negative the nonverbal reaction, such as displaying emotions of sadness, fear, anger, disgust, or contempt. If *JF* is zero, it suggests the expressions are neutral, or the number of dimensions that are positive reactions are the same as the number of dimensions that are negative reactions (Janis & Fadner, 1949). This measure reflects the BET approach of nonverbal communication, where the emotional valence of the reaction to stimuli is important. By capturing the strength of emotional reaction, the measure can suggest the degree to which broadcasters are reacting to stimuli.

These two conceptualizations and measures will be used as dependent variables throughout the study in order to examine two dimensions of the concept of nonverbal communication, through the lens of both BET theory and BECV theory. By adopting measures of both dimensions, theoretical connections between nonverbal fields and crisis journalism can be more thoroughly assessed.

Conclusion

In conclusion, it is important that researchers studying nonverbal communication, particularly in contexts outside of communication studies, recognize the already established definitions, types, conceptualizations, and measurements of nonverbal theories, especially because of the internal disagreements about them among nonverbal scholars. This is critical for a shared meaning and understanding among scholars, and this work hopes to provide a foundation upon which other media scholars could build nonverbal study in journalism and mediated contexts. The next chapter will explore ways in which media scholars have previously explored nonverbal communication and its connection to neutrality norms.

References

Birdwhistell, R. L. (1970). *Kinesics and context: Essays on body motion communication.* University of Pennsylvania Press.

Burgoon, J. K., Birk, T., & Pfau, M. (1990). Nonverbal behaviors, persuasion, and credibility. *Human Communication Research, 17,* 140–169.

Cohen, J. F., Ambadar, Z., & Ekman, P. (2007). Observer-based measurement of facial expression with the Facial Action Coding System. In J. A. Coan & J. J. B. Allen (Eds.), *Handbook of emotion elicitation and assessment.* Oxford University Press.

Crivelli, C., & Fridlund, A. J. (2019). Inside-out: From basic emotions theory to behavioral ecology view. *Journal of Nonverbal Behavior, 125,* 1–34.

Ekman, P. (1984). Expression and the nature of emotion. In K. Scherer & P. Ekman (Eds.), *Approaches to emotion* (pp. 319–344). Erbaum.

Ekman, P. (1999). Basic emotions. In T. Dalgleish & M. Power (Eds.), *Handbook of cognition and emotion* (pp. 45–60). John Wiley & Sons Ltd.

Ekman, P., & Friesen, W. V. (1969). Nonverbal leakage and clues to deception. *Psychiatry, 32*(1), 88–106.

Ekman, P., & Friesen, W. V. (1972). *Emotions in the human face: Guidelines for research and an integration of findings.* Pergamon Press.

Ekman, P., & Friesen, W. V. (1976). Measuring facial movement. *Environmental Psychology and Nonverbal Behavior, 1,* 56–75.

Fridlund, A. J. (2002). The behavioral ecology view of smiling and other facial expressions. In M. H. Abel (Ed.), *Mellen studies in psychology, Vol. 4. An empirical reflection on the smile* (pp. 45–82). Edwin Mellen Press.

Fridlund, A. J. (2017). The behavioral ecology view of facial displays, 25 years later. In J.-M. Fernández-Dols & J. A. Russell (Eds.), *Oxford series in social cognition and social neuroscience. The science of facial expression* (pp. 77–92). Oxford University Press.

Hall, J. A., & Knapp, M. L. (2013). *Nonverbal communication.* De Gruyter Mouton.

Janis, I. L., & Fadner, R. (1949). Coefficients of imbalance. In H. Laswell, N. Leites & Associates (Eds.), *Language of politics: Studies in quantitative semantics* (pp. 153–189). Stewart.

Knapp, M., & Hall, J. (2002). *Nonverbal Communication in Human Interaction.* Belmont, CA: Wadsworth.

Matsumoto, D. (2006). Culture and nonverbal behavior. In V. Manusov & M. L. Patterson (Eds.), *Handbook of nonverbal communication* (pp. 219–235). Sage.

Matsumoto, D., Frank, M. G., & Hwang, H. (Eds.). (2012). *Nonverbal communication: Science and applications.* Sage Publications.

Patterson, M. L. (2019). A systems model of dyadic nonverbal interaction. *Journal of Nonverbal Behavior, 43,* 111–132.

Reitzel, A., Yee, K., & Moran, R. (2023). Channels of nonverbal communication. ASCCC Open Education Resources Initiative (OERI). https://socialsci.libretexts .org/Bookshelves/Communication/Interpersonal_Communication/Interpersonal _Communication%3A_Context_and_Connection_%28OERI%29/05%3A_ Nonverbal_Elements_of_Communication/5.05%3A_The_Channels_of_Nonverbal _Communication

Ross, H. (2008). Proven strategies for addressing unconscious bias. *CDO Insights, 2*(5), 1–18.

Welch, J. (2019). Nonverbal "charades:" Teaching the power of emotion in public speaking. *Carolinas Communication Annual, 35,* 140–145.

Wrench, J. S., Punyanut-Carter, N. A., & Thweatt, K. S. (2020). *Interpersonal communication – A mindful approach to relationships.* SUNY New Paltz & SUNY Oswego via OpenSUNY. https://socialsci.libretexts.org/@go/page/66567

3 Nonverbal neutrality norm

The reporter stands in front of the family connection center in Columbine, Colorado, describing how parents are waiting to hear whether their child is among the shooting victims. In the background, parents are hugging their children, sobbing and shaking in fear. But mid-way through her report, the journalist's voice hitches, getting choked up at the emotional scene. She quickly slaps her hand to her mouth, unable to continue the report, and turns from the camera apologizing. The shot quickly goes to two stunned anchors, who appear uncomfortable. The lead anchor tells the reporter to "take time to get yourself together," and goes on to explain the shooting events in as calm and unemotional a way as possible.

This real-life reporting description from Columbine High describes the tension between reporting crises and maintaining neutrality norms. Most people could probably relate to the reporter's emotions, understanding that witnessing this tragedy could be overwhelming for anyone. Yet, the journalist's reactions – apologizing, turning away, cutting away from the reporter, and the anchors encouraging her to collect herself – suggest the challenging relationship between nonverbal neutrality, emotional displays, and professional norms of objectivity. This chapter will explain nonverbal communication's place in media research.

Nonverbal communication research in journalism scholarship

While literature on journalists' nonverbal expression is limited, the existing scholarship utilizes assumptions from either an individual-level approach similar to BET, or a social-level approach similar to BECV, but without ever formally citing these nonverbal theories.

Media effects scholars have found links between a reporter's expressiveness and the audiences' perception of the journalist's competency, caringness, trustworthiness, credibility, bias, and performance evaluation (Deavours, 2020a; Haumer & Donsbach, 2009; Burgoon et al., 1990). Additionally, studies find journalists' nonverbal factors have the ability to influence an audience's perceptions of future risk, political efficacy to resolve future crises,

DOI: 10.4324/9781003375340-3

and likelihood to support political causes (Deavours, 2020a; Kepplinger & Donsbach, 1987). These findings suggest the effects of nonverbal behavior are significant enough to warrant further investigation into the norms and practices of nonverbal communication of broadcasters. Some of the seminal works in this area are detailed below.

Babad (1999) explored the preferential treatment of broadcast journalists interviewing candidates for Israeli prime minister. The study found all six interviewers demonstrated preferential treatment of interview subjects through their nonverbal behavior. In addition, when comparing one veteran broadcast journalist's nonverbal behavior in interviewing the two opposing PM candidates, Babad found the broadcaster displayed favorable, positive nonverbal cues for the candidate he personally liked over 60% of the time, while the broadcaster displayed unfavorable, negative nonverbal cues for the other candidate that the broadcaster did not personally support 60% of the time; the extremes in the valences suggest a large difference in the nonverbal treatment of interview subjects. Babad explains the potential reasons for this variability in nonverbal presentation from a BET perspective – that there are universal expressions of bias and feelings when an interviewer does not agree with the interviewee. Babad's study was among the first to point to the nonverbal behavior of journalists as a potential source of bias.

In their study of the reactions of presidential candidates during debates, Bucy and Newhagen (1999) used a theoretical basis of emotional appropriateness heuristic, which suggests receivers are expecting certain types of nonverbal displays in certain contexts; when those expectations are violated by the speaker, the interpretation of that display, and thus its communicator, is negative. The researchers found this negative interpretation affected perceptions of credibility as well. This is largely consistent with a BECV-level approach, as the speakers are altering expressions based on audience expectations.

Seiter and colleagues (2009) in their experiment on candidate agreement/ disagreement during televised debates utilized Goffman's impression management theory, which states people try to control their nonverbal behavior to create the best impression of themselves. When candidates failed to agree with other candidates, they were seen as violating social norms of civility, and were thus rated less positively by audiences. The connection between normative expectations from within the profession and by audiences seems consistent with BECV frameworks.

Zimmerman (2014) completed a content analysis of everyday coverage of the nonverbal communication of broadcast journalists in the Las Vegas television market. Zimmerman uses assumptions that implicitly support both a BET and a BECV approach without directly citing either. First, Zimmerman (2014) suggests local journalists display nonverbal behaviors that match the tone or nature of the story; for instance, "if there was a sad story then the reporters for the most part, maintained an angry or neutral or sad expression" (p. 86). This would point to typifications of work, where the types or topics of stories presented would lead to differences in nonverbal behaviors. Zimmerman (2014) suggests the journalists are "operating under the influence of someone above them; perhaps news consultants, news directors, or general managers of the stations" (p. 89), another social-level influence. Yet, Zimmerman notes this facial expression matching was especially true for local journalists, while national journalists tended to be more detached and neutral in their presentations. Zimmerman suggests this is likely because local journalists have more of an emotional connection to the communities in which they work and likely live; this is more of an individual-level and psychological reaction-based assumption, consistent with BET.

In their content analysis of 9/11 coverage, Coleman and Wu (2006) utilize assumptions consistent with both BET and BECV, without explicitly citing them. They found broadcasters displayed significantly more nonneutral behavior than neutral behavior, and the difference in nonverbal neutrality valence changed depending on which stage of coverage journalists were reporting in, relying on Graber's (2002) stages of crisis coverage theory as the theoretical explanation. Coleman and Wu (2006) suggest journalists' vicarious traumatization, where journalists are emotionally impacted by trauma around them, causes emotional leakage at the individual level, leading to more pronounced displays of emotion than typical neutrality norms would allow. This conclusion is consistent with a psychological and individual-based explanation, like BET. Yet, consistent with BECV assumptions, Coleman and Wu (2006) also discuss the typification of work patterns within each of the three stages of crisis coverage, suggesting some stages have patterns of work that allow for more inherent bias than others.

Takahashi and colleagues (2022) examined how broadcasters utilized interpersonal touch, another form of nonverbal communication called haptics, during their disaster reporting during Hurricane Maria in Puerto Rico. They found broadcasters described using touch, either consciously or unconsciously, for the purposes of engagement and participation, empathy and caring, easing tension, and collective empowerment. However, they found journalists who were fulfilling roles more focused on objectivity, such as disseminator and interpretive roles, were less likely to use touch for fear of appearing too affective in their presentations. This suggests journalists who strive to maintain neutrality norms may be less willing to utilize emotional nonverbal communication tactics.

This study seeks to build on this previous scholarship. While most previous literature has focused on the media effects of journalists' nonverbal behavior on audiences, which provides a necessary justification for studying nonverbal presentation in news, this study approaches questions about nonverbal communication in journalistic work from the perspective of media sociology. Specifically, it examines how individual- and social-level influences of production predict the variability of broadcasters' nonverbal neutrality during crisis coverage. The normative concepts of neutrality and objectivity in professional journalism and their relationships to nonverbal communication are discussed next.

Journalism, objectivity, and neutrality

Scholars have sometimes called journalism a "profession in a permanent process of becoming" (Deuze & Witschge, 2017, p. 13). Professional norms and practices change with new technology, business models, and audience expectations (Stevens & Fuller, 2017). One norm that continually shifts in journalism systems across the world is objectivity.

In early American journalism, objectivity was synonymous with neutrality, a complete absence of personal values, opinions, or emotions in order to transmit the "truth" and facts (Schudson, 1990). This view is often referred to as a "mirrored reality," where journalists seek to produce reflections of the world around them, working to prevent distortions by not including personal emotions or beliefs (Vos, 2011).

Yet, most realize this was something merely to aspire to, too difficult, if not impossible, to put into everyday practice. Every choice of a journalist, from which stories to pursue to what sources to use, involves some level of subjectivity (Tuchman, 1972). The norm of objectivity later shifted from a focus on pure neutrality to an emphasis on balance to find truth (Durham, 1998). Even that definition becomes suspect, though, when viewed in postmodern interpretations of truth, where news is a social construction based on sociological factors, rather than a mirrored reflection of reality. Despite the theoretical knowledge that complete neutrality and objectivity are impossible, and perhaps (from the postmodern perspective) even undesirable standards, "the underlying principles of objectivity nonetheless remain firmly entrenched in the industry" (Reese, 1990, p. 393).

Today, objectivity is "at once a moral ideal, a set of reporting and editing practices, and an observable pattern of news writing" (Schudson, 2001, p. 149). The norm is supported explicitly in codes of ethics, textbooks, and organizational policies; it is also implicitly found in the ways journalists talk of their work, discuss the ideals and goals of the profession, and produce news (Schudson, 2001; Deavours, 2022). Tuchman (1972) described objectivity as a "strategic ritual," helping journalists mitigate continual pressures such as deadlines, possible libel suits, and anticipated punishments by managers by being able to claim adherence to objective practices. Objectivity is an "agent of legitimization" (Tuchman, 1978), a way of distinguishing between professional and novice reporters of events. Schudson (2001) also describes objectivity as an efficient form of production and a socialization tool, a way to describe the ideals of social practice in the field of journalism in order to maintain power over subordinates and to share group culture to new hires. These benefits of objective standards of reporting support its continuation as a professional norm.

Objectivity is the broader umbrella term for the normative standard, but part of that concept is the narrower term of neutrality. Heikkilä (2008) defines neutrality as a way to safeguard one's position in presentations to others. Neutrality in early American journalism was defined strictly as showing no stance or opinion on any subject while reporting, which aligned with the more political stance of nonalignment in regards to diplomacy or war (Heikkilä, 2008). More modern definitions of neutrality suggest it involves the reporter removing overt personal beliefs and emotions from the report (Kotišová, 2019).

Yet, research also finds journalism is not wholly unemotional. Most journalists believe emotion is a key part of storytelling, so journalists often struggle to find ways to incorporate emotions in professionally acceptable ways (Deavours, 2022). Wahl-Jorgensen (2020) finds emotion is widely present in award-winning journalism, and it is often cited as the reason for winning. Wahl-Jorgensen (2020) calls for an "emotional turn" in journalism studies to focus on the ways in which journalistic production, texts, and audience engagements focus on emotion. She suggests crisis reporting is a key battleground for emotional turn study, given the emotional labor of these trauma situations. While not all nonverbal behaviors share affective display, nonverbal cues are often key emotion communicators, making the study of nonverbal communication critical in this call for a journalistic emotional turn.

Nonverbal neutrality norm

In one of the first studies to discuss the normative implications of nonverbal neutrality, I interviewed 25 U.S. journalists who visually appeared in crisis reports (digital, podcast, televised broadcasts) about how they define and negotiate the boundaries of nonverbal neutrality (Deavours, 2022). Respondents did not originally mention nonverbal communication when discussing the ideals of the profession, which overwhelmingly upheld objectivity as a standard of practice; yet, once they began to discuss nonverbal behaviors, they connected nonverbal displays to neutrality, citing them as potentially negatively biasing audiences. Every participant upheld the need to remain nonverbally neutral.

The nonverbal neutrality norm was also a professional indicator. While they were able to empathize with reporters having to deal with emotional scenes, respondents felt trauma was a normal part of the job, and suggested that journalists who wanted to be successful would have to learn how to appear strong and neutral despite the emotionality of crises. They talked about emotional control, something they couldn't articulate how they did, as a critical part of "getting the job done."

However, they named particular instances where they were more willing to "give a pass" to journalists displaying nonneutral nonverbal behaviors, such as events with a lot of deaths or that involved children; yet respondents in providing this gray space of neutrality continued to insist on a quick return to neutrality standards. Journalists also indicated that political stories should have the highest levels of nonverbal neutrality, given the potential to bias audiences in political thought through nonverbal cues.

The respondents reported never receiving training in college or in newsrooms on how to regulate nonverbal neutrality. The only times they had considered nonverbal behavior in their reports were in negative norm violation conversations with managers or consultants, such as being told they were smiling too much, talking too fast, or dressing wrong. These reports indicate most journalists only encounter discussions of nonverbal communication when they violate a norm, suggesting the nonverbal neutrality norm is socially and observationally learned and enacted autonomically. This study suggests that, while journalists are willing to include emotion from sources and recognize the emotional labor of reporting during crises, they uphold nonverbal neutrality as a norm of the profession, despite having little to no training or feedback on how to do this.

It is important to continue to explore these normative boundary negotiations as they provide insight into the shared meaning and acceptance of these norms for journalists. This study extends discussions of norms of neutrality to nonverbal communication practices as well, by applying concepts of neutrality from journalism scholarship to the two dominant paradigms of nonverbal theory discussed in Chapter 2.

Remaining neutral during crisis

The media play a major role during crisis events, especially in terms of the public's emotional reaction to the events, making adherence to or deviation from neutrality norms particularly important to explore. Nonverbal researchers suggest a speaker's nonverbal communication during a crisis or heightened threat can have a strong impact on listeners' interpretations of the event, and political and social leaders' nonverbal communication can act as motivational cues for audiences on how they should be reacting to and interpreting unfolding events (Bucy, 2010). Therefore, it is important to research the degree of neutrality in reports during crisis events. By examining the adherence to or deviance from the norm of neutrality during crisis news coverage, researchers can understand the patterns of newsmaking decisions made during times of crisis and examine the product of either adhering to or deviating from a professional norm.

Graber (2002) found that these functions manifest variably across time during the reporting of a crisis story, and can affect degree of neutrality during coverage. Accordingly, she developed the stages of crisis coverage theory. Graber suggests there is more inherent bias in crisis coverage, but that the level of bias may change given certain influences, especially the "stage" or chronological time order of the report, an indication that journalists follow certain patterns of behavior through social-level norms and expectations, a BECV approach to nonverbal communication. However, the stages of crisis coverage theory dealt with written bias, not nonverbal bias. Therefore, Coleman and Wu (2006) applied Graber's theory to the nonverbal neutrality of broadcaster expressions during crisis coverage.

Coleman and Wu (2006) empirically tested Graber's stages of crisis coverage theory with their content analysis of the nonverbal behavior of broadcast journalists during 9/11 coverage. They analyzed the nonverbal neutral behavior of journalists in each of the three stages. Overall, they found broadcasters communicated significantly more positive or negative nonverbal expressions than neutral expressions during the 24-hour coverage period. They also found variability in nonverbal neutrality by stage. Yet, they also introduced the idea that journalists may be reacting individually and emotionally to trauma, losing control of their neutral nonverbal behaviors and displaying emotional leakage (Ekman & Friesen, 1969); this discussion introduced an interplay between individual, BET-level explanations and nonverbal neutrality variability as well as social, BECV-level approaches, but it wasn't empirically tested in the study.

In the original pilot study of this publication, I examined the nonverbal behaviors of broadcasters during the Sandy Hook Elementary School shooting (Deavours, 2020b). Drawing on the stages of crisis coverage theory from Graber (2002) and Coleman and Wu's (2006) nonverbal behavior additions, I conducted a content analysis of the nonverbal variability of broadcasters during the first 24 hours of the event. As with previous studies, I found broadcasters were more nonneutral than neutral in their nonverbal communication, but unlike Graber (2002) and Coleman and Wu (2006), there was no significant difference between stages. Based on Coleman and Wu's discussion of the emotional labor journalists carry out while covering a crisis, I began to explore other factors in both individual and social levels of influence.

Because of these potential effects, the coverage patterns built by journalists' neutrality choices, and the ubiquity of nonverbal behavior, the nonverbal neutrality of journalists should be further explored to increase understanding of normative behaviors during crisis coverage, and how this comes about. The next chapter will explore potential influences at various levels of influence (Shoemaker & Reese, 2014) on broadcasters' nonverbal variability.

References

Babad, E. (1999). Preferential treatment in television interviewing: Evidence from nonverbal behavior. *Political Communication, 16*, 337–358.

Bucy, E. P. (2010). Nonverbal communication, emotion, and political evaluation. In K. Doveling, C. von Scheve, and E. A. Konijn (Eds.), *The Routledge handbook of emotions and mass media* (pp. 195–220). Routledge.

Bucy, E. P., & Newhagen, J. E. (1999). The emotional appropriateness heuristic: Processed televised presidential reactions to the news. *Journal of Communication, 49*(4), 59–79.

Burgoon, J. K., Birk, T., & Pfau, M. (1990). Nonverbal behaviors, persuasion, and credibility. *Human Communication Research, 17*, 140–169.

Coleman, R., & Wu, D. (2006, June 7). More than words alone: Incorporating broadcasters' nonverbal communication into the stages of crisis coverage theory –evidence from September 11. *Journal of Broadcasting & Electronic Media, 50*(1), 1–17.

Deavours, D. (2020a, August). Visual framing effects of nonverbal communication in crisis. Association of Education in Journalism and Mass Communication (AEJMC): Electronic News Division Paper Panel [virtual conference due to COVID-19].

Deavours, D. (2020b). Written all over their faces: Bias and nonverbal expressions in Sandy Hook coverage. *Electronic News, 14*(3), 123–142.

Deavours, D. (2022). Nonverbal neutrality norm: How experiencing trauma affects journalists' willingness to display emotion. *Journal of Broadcast and Electronic Media, 67*(1), 112–134.

Deuze, M., & Witschge, T. (2017). Beyond journalism: Theorizing the transformation of journalism. *Journalism, 19*(2), 161–185.

Durham, M. (1998, May). On the relevance of standpoint epistemology to the practice of journalism: The case for 'strong objectivity.' *Communication Theory, 8*(2), 117–140.

Ekman, P., & Friesen, W. V. (1969). Nonverbal leakage and clues to deception. *Psychiatry, 32*(1), 88–106.

Graber, D. (2002). *Mass media and American politics* (6th ed.). CQ Press.

Haumer, F., & Donsbach, W. (2009). The rivalry of nonverbal cues on the perception of politicians by television viewers. *Journal of Broadcasting & Electronic Media, 53*(2), 262–279.

Heikkilä, H. (2008). Neutrality. In *The international Encyclopedia of communication.* Wiley Online Library. https://doi.org/10.1002/9781405186407.wbiecn010

Kepplinger, H. M., & Donsbach, W. (1987). The influence of camera perspectives on perception of a politician by supporters, opponents, and neutral observers. In D. L. Paletz (Ed.), *Political communication research* (pp. 62–72). Ablex.

Kotišová, J. (2019). An introduction to crisis reporting: Setting out. In *Crisis reporters, emotions, and technology* (pp. 1–28). Palgrave Macmillan, Cham.

Reese, S. (1990). The news paradigm and the ideology of objectivity: A socialist at the Wall Street Journal. *Critical Studies in Mass Communication, 7*(4), 390–410.

Schudson, M. (1990). *Origins of the ideal of objectivity in the professions.* Garland.

Schudson, M. (2001). The objectivity norm in American journalism. *Journalism, 2*(2), 149–170.

Seiter, J. S., Weger Jr., H., Jensen, A., & Kinzer, H. J. (2009). The role of background behavior in televised debates: Does displaying nonverbal agreement and/or disagreement benefit either debater? *The Journal of Social Psychology, 150*(3), 278–300.

Shoemaker, P., & Reese, S. (2014). *Mediating the message in the 21st century: A media sociology perspective.* Routledge.

Stevens, J., & Fuller, G. (2017). Journalistic challenges of the public and private: Exploring professional and ethical norms. *Australian Journalism Review, 39*(1), 113–125.

Takahashi, B., Zhang, Q., Chavez, M., & Nieves-Pizarro, Y. (2022). Touch in disaster reporting: Television coverage before Hurricane Maria. *Journalism Studies, 23*(7), 818–839.

Tuchman, G. (1972). Objectivity as strategic ritual: An examination of newsmen's notions of objectivity. *American Journal of Sociology, 77*(4), 660–679.

Tuchman, G. (1978). Professionalism as an agent of legitimation. *Journal of Communication, 28*(2), 106–113.

Vos, T. P. (2011). "A mirror of the times": A history of the mirror metaphor in journalism. *Journalism Studies, 12*(5), 575–589.

Wahl-Jorgensen, K. (2020). An emotional turn in journalism studies? *Digital Journalism, 8*(2), 175–194.

Zimmerman, J. (2014). Media bias through facial expressions on local Las Vegas television news programs: A visual content analysis [master's thesis]. University of Nevada, Las Vegas.

4 Nonverbal neutrality influence factors

It is definitely a challenge to be interviewing someone who has just lost their child to a tragedy like a school shooting while they cry and break down in front of you. It's a delicate balance of trying to appear empathetic, while not displaying too much emotion that you'd be considered unprofessional. Meanwhile I'm choking back my own tears thinking about how I'd react if I were in this mother's position losing my daughter. It's a lot to process in your head while you're doing a job on air with the world there to watch and critique.

This quote from a broadcast journalist who covered the Majory Stoneman Douglas High School shooting in Parkland, Florida, exemplifies the various influences on journalists' work during crises. They must simultaneously work to negotiate professional standards of neutrality, wanting to appear "professional" and "unbiased," while also needing to appear human and empathetic; these are social-level constructions of what is considered "appropriate" nonverbal behavior during a tragedy. Simultaneously, they are experiencing their own vicarious traumatization, witnessing and experiencing tragedy alongside victims; this is an individual, physiological reaction to emotional stimuli.

This chapter will explore the various influences on journalists' nonverbal neutrality during crisis reporting. Applying them in a content analysis of school shooting coverage from 1999 to 2018, the following chapters seek to better understand the ways in which both individual- and social-level influences shape nonverbal communication for broadcasters.

Interplay of influences

The use of multiple levels of analysis is common in media sociology studies as scholars seek to understand influences on professional practice. In their *Hierarchy of Influences on Media Messages*, Shoemaker and Reese (2014) acknowledge the importance of journalists' agency at the individual level in influencing the media content they produce, while also acknowledging that this agency is structured by assumptions at higher-order sociological levels

DOI: 10.4324/9781003375340-4

such as routines, organizational, extra-media, and cultural levels. Such a model helps scholars understand the "interplay between structure and agency, between actions people take and the conditions under which they act that are not of their own making" (Shoemaker & Reese, 2014, p. 11).

According to the assumptions of the two nonverbal theories of BET and BECV, both individual-level and social-level variables shape nonverbal behavior and communication. Additionally, both Graber's stages of crisis coverage theory (2002) and Coleman and Wu's discussion of nonverbal neutrality (2006) suggest broadcasters are experiencing an interplay between these influences while performing nonverbally.

First, at the individual level, journalists who are exposed to traumatic stimuli while covering a crisis have psychological, emotional reactions to the events, which in turn produce autonomic, uncontrolled nonverbal presentations about what they are experiencing. The severity (age of victims and number of deaths) and proximity (physically, emotionally, and chronemically) of crisis are considered variables that affect the intensity of the psychological reaction to an event, which could in turn influence the degree to which a journalist can control their nonverbal behavior.

Second, at the social level of influence, typifications of journalistic work encourage certain professional practices and standards, including how neutral the presentation of information about the event is. These typifications could be such strong influences on journalists' work that, even if experiencing psychological trauma, the journalist can fall into typified categories and routinized ways of doing their work, as the journalist maintains professional norms and boundaries. Typifications included in this analysis are roles performed, framing, topics of coverage, and sources used.

The study explores which factors influence broadcasters' nonverbal neutrality in crisis coverage. These independent variables are described in detail below.

Individual-level influences

At a micro-level, individual broadcast journalists have the ability to make decisions that shape journalistic work (Shoemaker & Reese, 2014). Individual characteristics, such as the gender and race of the journalists, have long been used as predictors for variability in reporting practices (e.g. Wagner, 2019). The individual level also becomes important when looking at normative values because the degree to which a norm is enacted or rejected happens at the individual journalist level (Shoemaker & Reese, 2014).

This interplay between individual influence and professional influence is important to examine in crisis reporting, especially given the potentially emotional nature of crisis. The situational contexts of these events often give journalists working in crisis more agency to act individually, outside of normative positions and values (Skovsgaard et al., 2013). Previous studies have found journalists experience deeply personal and overwhelmingly emotional reactions during crisis reporting. These reactions often happen live and are broadcast publicly, a deviation from the typical detached, unemotional, and neutral frame that defines the American reporting style (Kotišová, 2019). This study focuses on factors that the literature suggests are important in prompting individual-level, emotional effects on speakers and communication: the severity of the event, proximity to the event, and demographics. To be clear, these factors themselves do not reside at an individual level – rather they are conceptualized in this study as "individual level" because they are expected to be especially relevant in eliciting personal, emotional nonverbal responses, which suggest autonomous action by individual journalists.

Severity

The perceived severity of an event is important because it has effects on those on the scene and their communication strategies. The more severe the crisis is perceived as being, the greater the risk perception, the likelihood of emotionally reacting to it, and the likelihood that individuals will take action to protect themselves from that risk in the moment and for similar events in the future (Zhao et al., 2019). The perception of the severity of an event can affect the emotional reaction of those on the scene.

In a 2010 study of students who experienced a school shooting, Suomalainen and colleagues (2010) found that, the more severe a school shooting is, the more likely an individual exposed to the event will experience signs of distress. Communication strategies also change depending on the level of severity of the crisis (Xu & Li, 2012).

Since BET suggests nonverbal behaviors are the result of psychological reactions to stimuli (Ekman, 1999), the more severe a crisis is perceived to be by the broadcaster, the more likely it is that broadcasters will display more noticeable and more valenced nonverbal behaviors in their presentation of the information. As the perceived severity of the event increases, the harder it will be for journalists to control their nonverbal behaviors, meaning those behaviors will begin to be evident despite a communicator's best efforts to conceal them resulting in "emotional leakage" (Ekman & Friesen, 1969).

Severity is defined by two factors in this study. First, Xu and Li (2012) defined severity as the number of deaths and harm done during the event (Xu & Li, 2012) with more severe crises involving higher death rates. Second, previous research has also found a relationship between the age of victims of violence and the perceived event severity, where crimes involving younger children are considered more severe (Rogers & Davies, 2007). Within the field of journalism, events tend to be more newsworthy with higher rates of death, and where the perpetrator(s) and victims are young (Silva & Capellan, 2017). Therefore:

H1: The younger the age group of the victims in the event, the less neutral the nonverbal behavior of broadcast journalists will be immediately following the crisis.

H2: The more deaths from the event, the less neutral the nonverbal behavior of broadcast journalists will be immediately following the crisis.

Proximity

Proximity to an event is also an important factor in psychological reactions to crisis. Previous studies define proximity by three factors: physical distance, emotional distance (or the feeling of being closely related to the communities experiencing the crisis), and chronemic distance (or time from start of event) (Huang et al., 2015). Generally speaking, the more proximal that individuals are to a crisis, the more likely individuals are to seek information about, have emotional reactions to, and be affected by the crisis (Huang et al., 2015).

Proximity is also a factor in risk assessment; the closer someone is physically, timewise, or emotionally to the event, the more likely they are to consider the event to be personally risky. In one study, researchers found that physical distance from a threat during active shooter crises also affects the person's perception of message credibility (Egnoto et al., 2016), which could affect the ways journalists close to the scene take in and then deliver information about the active crisis.

Communication strategies also change depending on proximity, with people closer to the event being more willing to share and seek information (Huang et al., 2015). Berger and Luckmann (1966) suggest that the more "real" a subject becomes, the more the speaker will participate in a "continuous reciprocity of expressive acts," mirroring the subject's reactions; the researchers suggest this is known as showing "subjectivity emphatically 'close'" (p. 43) to that of those the speaker encounters.

Therefore, as a reporter gets closer both physically and emotionally to those experiencing trauma, their expressions will likely be affected as well. As individuals get closer to the crisis event, whether physically, socially, or chronemically, they may lose the ability to control their nonverbal behaviors as they become overwhelming, leading to "emotional leakage" in displays (Ekman & Friesen, 1969).

Physical proximity

In terms of physical distance, crisis scholars suggest that the closer physically a person is to the crisis stimuli, the more likely it is that the crisis will affect them psychologically (Huang et al., 2015). As they become more affected by the stimuli, BET suggests the individual will be less likely to control emotional displays. Therefore:

H3: The closer a journalist is physically to the location of the crisis scene, the less neutral their nonverbal behavior will be immediately following the crisis.

Emotional proximity

In terms of emotional proximity, researchers suggest that the more personally involved a person is in the event and the community being affected, the more likely they will be to experience psychological reactions to the trauma (Berger & Luckman, 1966; Zimmerman, 2014). Since BET suggests that nonverbal behaviors are the result of psychological reactions to stimuli (Ekman, 1999), the more personally proxemic an event is to the broadcaster, the more likely it is that the broadcaster will be unable to control their nonverbal behavior, leading to the emotional leakage of nonneutral nonverbal behaviors (Ekman & Friesen, 1969).

Journalism researchers have found that local journalists, who have worked continuously in a community that is undergoing crisis, will experience more emotional effects of covering crisis in their home areas compared to national correspondents who are unfamiliar with the area and its population (Zimmerman, 2014). Yet, like severity, there has been little research done specifically on the nonverbal behavior of journalists who are more or less proximal to the crisis event. Therefore:

H4: Local journalists will be less neutral in their nonverbal behaviors than national journalists immediately following the crisis.

Chronemic proximity

In terms of chronemic proximity, though, crisis researchers suggest that the relationship between how far away timewise a crisis worker is from an event and their emotional reaction to the event is not linear. Immediately following an event, a crisis worker will be able to perform routine tasks necessary for work, often called "triaging." Yet, as the situation progresses, the crisis worker will become overwhelmed with tragedy around them and begin to experience symptoms of vicarious traumatization, such as the "emotional leakage" of nonverbal behavior. As the worker is able to maintain more control over those emotions and symptoms of vicarious traumatization, they will be more likely to return to normal work patterns (Collins & Long, 2003).

Graber's (2002) stages of crisis coverage theory also suggests that the emotional impact of the events would vary as a function of time passed where vicarious traumatization would be delayed as journalists in the first hours of coverage work to find information and do their jobs; yet, by the second stage, the journalists would become strongly affected by the emotional toll of the event, causing more emotional leakage. By the third stage, the furthest time proximity from the event, the journalist would collect themselves and continue reporting according to their typical (and typified) practice.

This inverted U effect of chronemic proximity to crisis has been studied in many areas, including journalism (Coleman & Wu, 2006; Graber, 2002) and provides an outline of the psychological reactions of workers in crisis. Therefore:

H5: The nonverbal behavior of journalists will follow an inverted U pattern, where reports at the beginning and end of the event will present more neutral nonverbal behaviors than those in the middle of the event.

Individual demographics

The demographic characteristics of the individual broadcast journalists could also influence their likelihood of reacting to stimuli in an expressive way. For decades, nonverbal scholars have explored the effects of gender and race as demographic factors on nonverbal behavior.

Gender

Nonverbal communication research suggests that the gender of the speaker affects the expressiveness of their nonverbal behavior. Meta-analysis has shown a strong tendency for females to be more facially expressive than males (Hall, 1984), but other research has shown these findings to be inconclusive (Hall et al., 2000).

In their studies on the nonverbal behavior of journalists in crisis coverage, Coleman and Wu (2006) studied the influence that gender has on the neutrality of nonverbal expression while reporting. The studies found that while female broadcasters were more likely to have slightly higher neutrality scores than male journalists, the results were not statistically significant. While these findings in recent journalism studies suggest gender may not have a main effect, the breadth of nonverbal research finding significant differences in gender begs further investigation in this study. Therefore:

H6: Female journalists will be less neutral in their nonverbal behaviors than male journalists immediately following the crisis.

Race

Racial differences in expressivity have also been studied with inconclusive results. Matsumoto's (1993) survey of the four most prevalent racial and ethnic groups in America found considerable differences in display rules and emotional expressions as a function of ethnicity; the findings suggest that, overall, whites were more likely to consider the expression of negatively valenced emotions, such as contempt, disgust, fear, and sadness, as more appropriate than Asians, Black, and Hispanics. Overall, whites were more likely to express themselves with negative expressions than minorities, and Black participants were the least likely to express themselves through negative emotions. Similar results were found by Vrana and Rollock (2010), whose study suggests Black students exhibited more positive facial expressions, while Whites were more negatively expressive; interestingly, the study also suggested Blacks were more autonomic in their emotional reactions, which they said suggested racial differences between Black and white nonverbal expressions and in the ability to control or conceal expressions as a reaction to stimuli. Additionally, researchers found that Asian populations are less likely to display emotional expressivity compared to whites, as a coping mechanism to stress and trauma reactions since emotionality is less aligned with Asian cultural values (Wang & Lau, 2018). This again suggests racial and ethnic differences in socioemotional processes.

There has not been enough research in these areas specific to broadcasters' nonverbal behavior. Broadcast newsrooms are dominated by white journalists with minorities comprising only a quarter of staffers (RTDNA, 2021), so most journalistic norms are based on predominantly white newsrooms, although there is hope for continued diversification of the industry. Therefore:

H7: Nonverbal behavior will vary significantly based on the race of the journalist.

Social-level influences on journalists' work: Typifications

The Behavioral Ecology View of Facial Displays (BECV) suggests nonverbal behaviors are not merely hard-wired, personal reactions to events that are universal and uncontrollable; there are also larger social structures and dynamics that constrain, channel, and enable an individual's nonverbal behavior. BECV scholars suggest that as the functions and expectations of social situations become more clear and routinized, the nonverbal behavior may occur without conscious thought about the social and situational influences (Fridlund, 2017; Patterson, 2019). BECV suggests nonverbal behaviors may follow a routinization pattern, where the outcomes of practice and behavior become almost taken-for-granted because they are the best tools for a particular circumstance, and they become so ingrained and ritualized into social practice that they practically become the "natural" way to react, even unconsciously.

Typifications of journalistic work are similar in their ability to become ritualized and taken-for-granted behaviors. Berkowitz (1992) describes typifications as the "classifications in which relevant characteristics are central to the solution of practice tasks or problems at hand and are constituted in and grounded in everyday activity" (p. 178). Typifications are ways that actors orient themselves to action in their situations. Typification "involves disregarding those individual differences of the typified objects that are not relevant to such a purpose" (McKinney, 1969, p. 1). Typifications keep journalists from having to report on every event as if it were completely unprecedented, which would require a journalist to invent new coverage strategies and practices every time something occurred. This would be cumbersome and inefficient as a work practice. Instead, typifications reduce uncertainty for both journalists and audiences, increase predictability, and make work more manageable.

Examples of typifications across crisis journalism include role performance, thematic and episodic framing, topics of coverage, and types of sourcing; this research will examine the variability of the nonverbal behavior of journalists across these professional typifications in order to better understand the potential influence of sociological patterns of nonverbal communication suggested by BECV.

Role performance

Many media sociologists have explored the influence that the typifications of journalistic roles have on adherence to norms during crisis. Roles are sets of expectations that classify the behaviors of people in certain positions in society (Weaver et al., 2019). Roles are typifications of expected behavior that are shaped at the macro- or meso-level of influence, but adopted at the routine and individual levels (Shoemaker & Reese, 2014; Hellmueller & Mellado, 2015).

Researchers suggest that the ways journalists think about their roles, called role conceptions, will shape the ways in which their stories are produced, as well as shaping the final product (Hellmueller & Mellado, 2015). As individuals adapt to new roles, they will model their behaviors to conform to the roles. However, research shows that what role journalists believe they are performing is not always congruent with the roles they actually perform when reporting (Mellado & Van Dalen, 2013). Therefore, it is important to study how the role is being enacted, called role performance, in terms of nonverbal behavior (Weaver et al., 2019; Hellmueller & Mellado, 2015).

Weaver, Willnat, and Wilhoit (2019) describe four types of roles for journalists – disseminator, interpreter, adversarial, and populist-mobilizer. Each role has different norms for how it is to be performed or enacted in routine practice. A journalist adopting a disseminator role emphasizes the fast relay of information to the public without commentary; neutrality is critically important in this role (Reynolds & Barnett, 2003; Weaver et al., 2019).

For interpretive journalists, the focus is on analyzing the complexity of the issue, addressing policies, and investigating official claims (Weaver & Wilhoit, 1991). It moves beyond the dissemination role to add commentary and interpretation. There may be more acceptance for nonneutrality in this role as journalists are more apt to share their experience as resources and eyewitnesses in this role (Weaver et al., 2019).

The adversarial role places the media as watchdog to business or officials, offering alternative viewpoints (Weaver & Wilhoit, 1991); research suggests this role is not as strong during crisis since there is an increased level of trust in officials during crisis (Graber, 2002). However, media could act as a watchdog for the government, protecting the country from outside influences, such as terrorists, enemy countries, or laws/policies that contribute to hurting the nation (Weaver & Wilhoit, 1991). This is considered the least neutral role because journalists are taking an active stance for and against entities (Reynolds & Barnett, 2003).

The populist-mobilizer role of media lets everyday people express their views, develops intellectual and cultural interests, motivates people to get involved, and points to possible solutions (Weaver et al., 2019). This role allows for more subjectivity, meaning there would be more acceptability for expressions of nonneutrality while enacting this role.

The concept of role performance is important to crisis coverage because it could suggest why the adherence to the norm fluctuates within the event coverage itself. BECV suggests that people change their nonverbal cues to reflect social norms or expectations of behavior, a transactional behavior rather than an uncontrollable one (Fridlund, 2017). Therefore, if a journalist is performing a role with an emphasis on, for example, being adversarial and taking sides, compared to a journalist who is being detached and facts-based (disseminator role), it would be expected that journalists' nonverbal neutrality would reflect the varied ways neutrality or nonneutrality are expressed through these professional roles.

In their national survey of U.S. journalists, Weaver, Willnat, and Wilhoit (2019) find the most neutral role is disseminator, followed by populist-mobilizer, interpretative, and adversarial as the least neutral role. Therefore:

H8: There will be a significant difference between the neutrality of journalists' behavior in performing different roles.

H8a: Broadcasters performing the disseminator role will be the most neutral nonverbally.

H8b: Broadcasters performing the adversarial role will be the least neutral nonverbally.

Thematic/episodic frames

Journalists rely on routine typifications of news frames as a way to make the unpredictable more manageable, turning even unique crisis events into the standard typifications of "what-a-story" or breaking/developing news coverage (Berkowitz, 1992). Iyengar (1991) outlines two of the more significant typified frames in news coverage: the episodic and thematic frames. Episodic frames are those that focus solely on one example, event, or individual (e.g. the facts of a particular school shooting). Thematic frames place the issues in a broader issue context (e.g. coverage of the proliferation of U.S. school shootings, gun control regulation, etc.).

Studies show journalists tend to cover crises episodically, focusing on the event and individuals rather than larger social or public issues (Iyengar, 1991). Previous studies suggest episodic framing tends to be more cognitively driven, focused on facts and information. Thematic framing tends to be more affectively focused, creating more emotion-laden conversations around the event's broader issues (Gross, 2008).

Even crisis events begin to use thematic framing early on in coverage, especially as similar events occur more frequently, and thematic coverage allows journalists to tie together patterns from the same kind of "what-a-story" events (McCluskey, 2016). Neutrality norms in journalism suggest that when providing facts about an event, a journalist would be expected to present that information in a nonbiased way, but interpretative or more emotionally driven content may encourage less neutral presentations (Cho et al., 2003; Graber, 2002; Coleman & Wu, 2006). Since BECV suggests that communicators would work to match their nonverbal behavior to the expectations of the message and receiver (Fridlund, 2017), this would suggest that episodic frames would lead to more neutral nonverbal presentations, while thematic frames would allow for more nonneutral nonverbal presentations. Therefore:

H9: Journalists framing information episodically will be more neutral nonverbally than journalists framing information thematically.

Topic

While thematic and episodic frames help to categorize the general content of crisis coverage, these frames can be broken down into typified topics as well. Nonverbal behavior researchers suggest nonverbal communication expectations can change based on topic, which people are socialized to, even in early childhood (Grebelsky-Lichtman, 2014). This suggests journalists may change their nonverbal communication encoding by topic as well, working to meet the expected styles and goals of addressing socially learned topic types through nonverbal frames.

Tuchman (1973) says variability in practice and the uncertainty and complexity of events in the journalists' world impede the routinization of work, so journalists create typifications of stories to decrease that uncertainty. Because these categories of story type are so routinized and taken for granted for journalists and audiences, they can be difficult to identify and describe. However, researchers can tease out primary topics by reviewing other crisis journalism studies.

In examining common topics from previous studies of school shootings (e.g. McCluskey, 2016; Silva & Capellan, 2017), this research utilizes four primary topic categories for school shooting coverage: (1) facts about the event, the shooter, the guns used, the scene and its investigation, and the conditions of victims; (2) policy issues, including gun laws, mental health regulation, and school safety measures; (3) reactions from the local community, the nation, and politicians; and (4) first-hand accounts from witnesses and survivors of the event. Little work has been done to identify the inherent neutrality of these topics, making a true hypothesis about the changing nonverbal neutrality by topic difficult. Instead:

RQ1: How do the topics of coverage affect the neutrality of nonverbal behavior of the broadcast journalist immediately following the crisis?

Sourcing

News sources are also a major influence on journalistic routines. "Source" in this context means the person or organization that is providing information from which the reporter is gathering material for a story. News is often defined as information provided by sources, typically officials of bureaucratic commercial organizations and professions, and is repackaged for general audiences by journalists (Gans, 1979). Speakers often attempt to present themselves differently based on who they are speaking to or about (DePaulo, 1992). As mentioned earlier, sociologists Berger and Luckmann (1966) suggest that subjects become more real face-to-face. This speaks to the self-presentation goals of BECV from a sociological perspective. This could potentially mean that as sourcing changes in crisis communication, so will the nonverbal behavior of journalists align with those speakers and the self-presentation expectations of that source type.

Previous research shows the sourcing decisions of journalists have the ability to influence frames or presentations of news content (Fisher, 2018), and journalists may follow the source's lead in framing news content (Boesman et al., 2015). There is also a typification of sourcing, where journalists most often utilize "legitimate" or official sources that support the status quo (Skovsgaard et al., 2013). There are other regularly used types of sources, such as experts, members of the affected community, victims of similar events, and even other media outlets or themselves as first-person witnesses. It is important to note, though, that journalists are also less likely to properly source information during crises, struggling to confirm certain details in the hectic environment and, therefore, not sourcing anyone at all (Graber, 2002).

While common types of sources in school shooting coverage have been identified by journalism scholars (McCluskey, 2016; Cho et al., 2003; Silva & Capellen, 2017), the relative expectations of those sources and journalistic neutrality need more exploration. Therefore:

RQ2: How does the type of source the broadcast journalist is citing affect the neutrality of nonverbal behavior of the broadcast journalist immediately following the crisis?

Graber's stages of crisis coverage theory

Graber's stages of crisis coverage theory provides a unique lens through which to examine BET and BECV influences on the nonverbal behavior of journalists in more detailed ways. Both Graber (2002) and Coleman and Wu (2006) discuss ways in which journalists' neutrality may vary across the time periods called "stages," creating patterns of behavior and influences that need to be further examined. In addition, Shoemaker and Reese's (2014) hierarchy of influences suggest that other influences could be shaped by social-level typifications, making the stages of coverage as a typification factor important to study across independent variables. Therefore:

RQ3: What interaction effects are there between individual-level influences and the three stages of crisis on the nonverbal neutrality of broadcasters?

RQ4: What interaction effects are there between social-level influences and the three stages of crisis on the nonverbal neutrality of broadcasters?

Each of these hypotheses and research questions will be measured through the *NNS* in order to understand the dimension of nonverbal expressiveness, as well as *JF* in order to understand the dimension of emotional valence of nonverbal reactions to the events. The next chapter will address the methodology used in addressing hypotheses and research questions.

References

Berger, P. L., & Luckmann, T. (1966). *The social construction of reality: A treatise in the sociology of knowledge*. Anchor Books.

Berkowitz, D. (1992). Routine newswork and the what-a-story: A case study of organizational adaptation. *Journal of Broadcasting & Electronic Media, 36*(1), 45–61.

Boesman, J. L., Berbers, A., d'Haenens, L., & Van Gorp, B. (2015). The news is in the frame: A journalist-centered approach to the frame-building process of the Belgian-Syrian fighters. Paper presented at the International Communication Association, Washington.

Cho, J., Boyle, M. P., Keum, H., Shevy, M. D., McLeod, D. M., Shah, D. V., & Pan, Z. (2003). Media, terrorism, and emotionality: Emotional differences in media content and public reactions to the September 11th terrorist attacks. *Journal of Broadcasting & Electronic Media, 47*(3), 309–327.

Coleman, R., & Wu, D. (2006, June 7). More than words alone: Incorporating broadcasters' nonverbal communication into the stages of crisis coverage theory – evidence from September 11. *Journal of Broadcasting & Electronic Media, 50*(1), 1–17.

Collins, S., & Long, A. (2003). Too tired to care? The psychological effects of working with trauma. *Journal of Psychiatric & Mental Health Nursing, 10*, 17–27.

DePaulo, B. M. (1992). Nonverbal behavior and self-presentation. *Psychological Bulletin, 111*(2), 203–243.

Egnoto, M. J., Griffin, D. J., Svetieva, E., & Winslow, L. (2016). Information sharing during the University of Texas at Austin active shooter/suicide event. *Journal of School Violence, 15*(1), 48–66.

Ekman, P. (1999). Basic emotions. In T. Dalgleish & M. Power (Eds.), *Handbook of cognition and emotion* (pp. 45–60). John Wiley & Sons Ltd.

Ekman, P., & Friesen, W. V. (1969). Nonverbal leakage and clues to deception. *Psychiatry*, *32*(1), 88–106.

Fisher, C. (2018). News sources and journalists'-source interaction. *Oxford research Encyclopedia of communication*. Oxford University Press. https://doi.org/10.1093/acreforce/9780190228613.013.849

Fridlund, A. J. (2017). The behavioral ecology view of facial displays, 25 years later. In J.-M. Fernández-Dols & J. A. Russell (Eds.), *Oxford series in social cognition and social neuroscience. The science of facial expression* (pp. 77–92). Oxford University Press.

Gans, H. J. (1979). The messages behind the news. *Columbia Journalism Review*, *17*(5), 40.

Graber, D. (2002). *Mass media and American politics* (6th ed.). CQ Press.

Grebelsky-Lichtman, T. (2014). Children's verbal and nonverbal congruent and incongruent communication during parent-child interactions. *Human Communication Research*, *40*(4), 415–441.

Gross, K. (2008). Framing persuasive appeals: Episodic and thematic framing, emotional response, and policy opinion. *Political Psychology*, *29*(2), 169–192.

Hall, J. (1984). *Nonverbal sex differences: Communication accuracy and expressive style*. John Hopkins University Press.

Hall, J., Carter, J., & Horgan, T. (2000). Gender differences in nonverbal communication of emotions. In A. Fischer (Ed.), *Gender and emotion: Social psychological perspectives*. Cambridge University Press.

Hellmueller, L., & Mellado, C. (2015). Professional roles and news construction: A media sociology conceptualization of journalists' role conception and performance. *Communication & Society*, *28*(3), 1–11.

Huang, Y. L., Starbird, K., Orand, M., Stanek, S. A., & Pedersen, H. T. (2015). Connected through crisis: Emotional proximity and the spread of misinformation online. *CSCW '15: Proceedings of the 18th ACM conference on computer supported cooperative work & social computing* (pp. 969–980). Vancouver, BC, Canada.

Iyengar, S. (1991). The media game: New moves, old strategies. *Press, Politics, and Political Science*, *9*(1), 1–6.

Kotišová, J. (2019). An introduction to crisis reporting: Setting out. In *Crisis reporters, emotions, and technology* (pp. 1–28). Palgrave Macmillan, Cham.

Matsumoto, D. (1993). Ethnic differences in affect intensity, emotion judgments, display rule attitudes, and self-reported emotional expression in an American sample. *Motivation and Emotion*, *17*(2), 107–123.

McCluskey, M. (2016). *News framing of school shootings: Journalism and American social problems*. Lexington Books.

McKinney, J.C. (1969). Typification, typologies, and sociological theory. *Social Forces*, *48*(1), 1–12.

Mellado, C., & Van Dalen, A. (2013). Between rhetoric and practice: Explaining the gap between role conception and performance in journalism. *Journalism Studies*, *15*(6), 859–878.

Patterson, M. L. (2019). A systems model of dyadic nonverbal interaction. *Journal of Nonverbal Behavior*, *43*, 111–132.

RTDNA. (2021, June). Local newsroom diversity reaches records, but representation gap shrinks slowly. https://www.rtdna.org/news/local-news-diversity-reaches-records-but-representation-gap-shrinks-slowly

Reynolds, A., & Barnett, B. (2003). 'America under attack': CNN's verbal and visual framing of September 11. In S. Chermak, F. Bailey, & M. Brown (Eds.), *Media representations of September 11* (pp. 85–102). Westport, CT: Praeger Press.

Rogers, P., & Davies, M. (2007). Perceptions of victims and perpetrators in a depicted child sexual abuse case gender and age factors. *Journal of Interpersonal Violence, 22*(5), 566–584.

Shoemaker, P., & Reese, S. (2014). *Mediating the message in the 21st century: A media sociology perspective.* Routledge.

Silva, J. R., & Capellen, J. A. (2017). The media's coverage of mass public shootings in America: Fifty years of newsworthiness. *International Journal of Comparative and Applied Criminal Justice, 43*(1), 77–97.

Skovsgaard, M., Albæk, E., Bro, P., & de Vreese, C. (2013). A reality check: How journalists' role perceptions impact their implementation of the objectivity norm. *Journalism, 14*(1), 22–42.

Suomalainen, L., Haravuori, H., Berg, N., Kiviruusu, O., & Marttunen, M. (2010). A controlled follow-up study of adolescents exposed to a school shooting – Psychological consequences after four months. *European Psychiatry, 26*(8), 490–497.

Tuchman, G. (1973). Making news by doing work: Routinizing the unexpected. *American Journal of Sociology, 79*(1), 110–131.

Vrana, S. R., & Rollock, D. (2010). The role of ethnicity, gender, emotional content, and contextual differences in physiological, expressive, and self-reported emotional responses to imagery. *Cognition and Emotion, 16*(1), 165–192.

Wagner, M. C. (2019). Journalists' gender and influence: Effects on the perceived severity of sexual harassment. *Cuadernos.info, 44*, 43–59.

Wang, S., & Lau, A. S. (2018). Ethnicity moderates the benefits of perceived support and emotional expressivity on stress reactivity for Asian Americans and Euro Americans. *Cultural Diversity and Ethnic Minority Psychology, 24*(3), 363–373.

Weaver, H., & Wilhoit, G. (1991). *The American Journalist: A portrait of US news people and their work* (2nd ed.). Indiana Press University.

Weaver, D., Willnat, L., & Wilhoit, G. (2019). The American journalist in the digital age: Another look at U.S. news people. *Journalism & Mass Communication Quarterly, 96*(1), 101–130.

Xu, K., & Li, W. (2012). An ethical stakeholder approach to crisis communication: A case study of Foxconn's 2010 employee suicide crisis. *Journal of Business Ethics, 117*(2), 371–386.

Zhao, M., Rosoff, H., & John, R. S. (2019). Media disaster reporting effects on public risk perception and response to escalating tornado warnings: A natural experiment. *Risk Analysis: An International Journal, 39*(3), 535–553.

Zimmerman, J. (2014). Media bias through facial expressions on local Las Vegas television news programs: A visual content analysis [master's thesis]. University of Nevada, Las Vegas.

5   Measuring nonverbal neutrality

To better understand the influences on broadcasters' nonverbal neutrality variability during crisis coverage, this study utilizes a content analysis of six of the deadliest school shootings to demonstrate how nonverbal neutrality norms could be studied in journalism contexts.

Method

Content analysis is used to determine the presence, meaning, and relationships among key concepts, words, images, structures, or themes in a source. The tool allows scholars to make inferences about the texts, sources, audiences or surrounding culture, social structures, and time period of the source. This research utilizes a systematic quantitative approach through Kaid and Wadsworth's (1989) seven-step method. Content analysis is an appropriate method to investigate the nonverbal behavior of broadcast journalists during crisis coverage as it allows for the examination of large volumes of real-world news content in a nonreactive and unobtrusive way (Holsti, 1969). Content analysis is particularly helpful for investigations when the subject's own language is crucial (Neuendorf, 2002), which is the case with the nonverbal communication of journalists.

Sampling

The context for this study is school shootings, for three main reasons. First, the coverage of school shootings holds an important place in journalism history as some of the highest rated live broadcasts of crises in America (Althaus, 2002). Second, school shootings are highly emotional due to the large death tolls of innocent and typically young victims, making these cases a good way to study the potential impact individual emotional reactions can have on the nonverbal behavior of journalists. Third, given the recent proliferation and extensive coverage of school shootings, there is evidence of the routinization of coverage of these events, making them a good case study for the influence of typifications (McCluskey, 2016).

DOI: 10.4324/9781003375340-5

This study draws samples from six case studies of school shooting coverage. For this study, the six deadliest shootings in United States history from 1999 to 2021 were chosen, as the severity and timeline of events are important concepts in the study. 1999 was chosen as the beginning point, in part because of Columbine's historical significance in the proliferation of school shootings in America, but also because of technological considerations of having 24/7 coverage of a crisis available on national broadcasts. While the University of Texas tower shooting, which happened in 1966, remains the third deadliest school shooting in American history, it was not included because the television broadcast coverage of the event was not similar enough to the live, uninterrupted coverage of those that occurred after 1999. The study was also conducted in 2020–2021 before the Robb Elementary School shooting in Uvalde, Texas, which at the time of this writing is the third deadliest school shooting in U.S. history with 22 deaths and 18 injuries; Uvalde is not included in these results because it occurred after data collection was complete. Each of the six cases from 1999 to 2021 is briefly described in chronological order below.

Columbine High School

The shootings at Columbine High School took place on April 20, 1999, in Columbine, Colorado. Two twelfth grade students, 18- and 17-years-old, shot 12 students and one teacher; 24 others were injured. Both shooters committed suicide on scene. At the time, it was the deadliest school shooting in American history, and at the time of this writing, it is the sixth deadliest in the U.S. Columbine also has significance in journalism history. It was one of the first school shootings to be covered live on broadcast television networks for continuous periods, setting the stage for how networks would cover school shootings in the future (Cullen, 2009). Columbine also serves as a truly unique coverage experience for most of the journalists who covered it, which makes it an interesting case to analyze within the larger timeline of school shootings.

Virginia Tech

The shootings at Virginia Tech took place on April 16, 2007. A senior at the college, then 23-years-old, shot and killed 32 people on the campus; 23 others were injured. The shooter shot himself. Virginia Tech is the deadliest school shooting in the history of the United States at the time of this writing. As well as being the most severe in terms of deaths, the coverage of Virginia Tech drew international attention and widespread criticism. Media debates about mental health, gun control, the responsibility of schools to protect students, and journalism ethics were ubiquitous, and after television news organizations aired portions of the killer's manifesto, many debated the media's role in covering school shootings (Maddox, 2007). Due to its severity and its part in sparking media debates on gun control, mental health, and journalism ethics during the coverage of the events, Virginia Tech is also an important case to study.

Sandy Hook Elementary School

The Sandy Hook Elementary School shooting occurred on December 14, 2012, in Newtown, Connecticut. A 20-year-old man shot and killed 26 people and injured two others. This included 20 children between the ages of six and seven, and six adult staff members. The shooter also killed his mother at their home. The shooter committed suicide. At this writing, the shooting is the deadliest mass shooting at an American primary school, and it is the second deadliest school shooting. The event prompted national petitions for gun control legislation. In addition, the State Attorney's report suggested that the shooter had Asperger's syndrome, prompting numerous media discussions about mental health and violence. Because of the severity of the event targeting primary school aged children and the renewed debate of media's role in covering school shootings, Sandy Hook is another important case for studying journalists' nonverbal behavior during school shooting coverage.

Umpqua Community College

The Umpqua Community College shooting occurred on October 1, 2015, at the UCC campus near Roseburg, Oregon. A 26-year-old student enrolled at the college shot a professor and eight students in a classroom, injuring eight others. The shooter committed suicide. Investigators suggest the case was almost classified as a religious hate crime because the shooter asked students their religion before shooting them, but officials didn't have enough evidence to classify the event (ADL, 2015); media coverage focused on the religious aspects of the case, as well as college preparedness plans. The event is the eighth deadliest shooting in American history at the time of this writing, and the third deadliest on a college campus after Virginia Tech and the University of Texas tower shootings. Because of its severity in deaths and similar ages of victims from Virginia Tech, the Umpqua shooting coverage is included as a case study.

Marjory Stoneman Douglas High School (Parkland)

The shooting at Marjory Stoneman Douglas High School in Parkland, Florida, took place on February 14, 2018. Just as the media did in its coverage of this event, this study used the shorthand of "Parkland" to refer to the shootings. The shooter shot and killed 17 people and injured 17 others. The shooter was arrested and pled guilty in exchange for a life sentence. The Parkland shootings are significant in the history of American school shootings for many reasons. First, there were many concerns about how law enforcement handled the incident prior to and after the shooting. Additionally, police response times were slower than usual in this case, sparking controversy. Importantly, Parkland survivors, primarily young students, founded Never Again MSD, an advocacy group that lobbies for legislative action on gun violence. The Never Again movement has sparked international attention and led to legislation for stricter gun laws in Florida (Cullen, 2019). The media attention given to Parkland was arguably among the largest coverage a single school shooting has received, partly because of the desire of victims to utilize media for gun control advocacy platforms (Cullen, 2019). In addition, the Parkland shooting is the deadliest high school shooting in the United States, and it is the fifth deadliest school shooting in American history at the time of this writing. Because of the severity in terms of the number of victims, the amount of media coverage received, and the intensified media focus on gun control policy, the Parkland shooting is an important case study.

Sante Fe High School

The shooting at Sante Fe High School occurred on May 18, 2018, in Santa Fe, Texas. A 17-year-old student at the school shot and killed ten people, including eight students and two teachers, and wounded 13 others. The shooter was arrested and charged with capital murder of multiple persons and aggravated assault. He was found to be unfit to stand trial for mental incompetence; if convicted, he faces a sentence of 40 years to life. The shooter's mental health was widely discussed by the media. However, compared to the Parkland shooting just three months prior to Sante Fe, the media coverage was not as prominent primarily because residents of Sante Fe largely declined to participate in media coverage and did not support gun control actions (Deutch, 2019). It is currently the seventh deadliest school shooting in the U.S. at the time of this writing, and the third deadliest at a high school. Because of its severity, the ability to contrast with other high school shootings, and the lesser media reaction after the event, the Sante Fe shootings provide a unique lens through which to examine the variability of broadcast journalists' nonverbal behavior during crisis coverage.

Units of analysis

Once the six case studies were selected, a sample was drawn from digital archive clips of the first 24 hours of coverage of these events from six national networks: ABC, CBS, NBC, MSNBC, CNN, and FOX News. These media outlets were chosen since they are the six highest rated televised broadcast news networks for these events. In addition, national broadcasters are the "gold standard" for the news profession, and their presentation styles are most likely to be influential and modeled by local journalists, which encourages profession-wide typification patterns.

For Columbine and Sandy Hook, the researcher collected archival clips for the first 24 hours of their coverage from various sources, including the networks directly, archival sites like Vanderbilt TV News Archive, and archivists willing to share their files. Complete televised coverage for these events has yet to be reliably archived on digital libraries for public use, making it necessary to use different collection methods for these cases compared to the last four. In addition, very little local broadcast coverage is accessible for researchers, again reinforcing the need to sample only national broadcast networks for this study. For Sandy Hook, Umpqua, Parkland, and Sante Fe, the archival footage was gathered and viewed from the website Internet Archive (2020), a digital library service for news clips and other historical material from 2009 to today. For each of the six case studies, a search was conducted for the school shooting's name ("Sandy Hook," "Umpqua," "Parkland," and "Sante Fe"); the date range was the day of the shooting and the day after.

Only the first 24 hours were coded based on Graber's (2002) stages of crisis coverage theory's focus on the short-term reactions of journalists after a crisis. This time period was utilized by Coleman and Wu's (2006) and Xigen, Lindsay, and Mogensen's (2002) analyses of 9/11 coverage, as well as my (2020b) pilot study of school shooting coverage.

The sample unit was defined as a 15-minute digital clip from the network coverage, the common ratings measure in television. This generates four possible sample units each hour and 96 total for the 24-hour period per network. Since the sample included six networks, there are a total of 576 sample units in the population for each event. There are six case studies or school shooting events, meaning the total population for this study is 3,456 sample units.

From the total population of sample units, a stratified random sample was drawn so that an equal number of sample clips from each of the six case studies were chosen, as well as an equal distribution of networks and time periods. Since there are four possible sample units per network per hour, the researcher randomly selected one sample unit from each network every two hours. Two hours was chosen as a way to restrict the dataset, making analysis manageable, without losing analysis across time periods and stages. This provided a total of 12 sample units per network for each event. Multiplied by six networks, this provided 72 sample units per event, and with six case study events, this generated 432 sample units.

However, archiving issues and coverage patterns did not allow the researcher to collect all 432 sample units. Columbine had 52 sample units, primarily due to a lack of available digital archives; Virginia Tech had 33 sample units for the same reasons. Sandy Hook had 59 sample units, and the missing sample units were primarily because the networks did not cover the event continuously or even have break-ins to regular programming for all sampling periods. The same was true for Umpqua, which had 62 sample units; Parkland, which had 67 sample units; and Santa Fe, which had 52 sample units. The coverage of Santa Fe was notably lower than other post-2012 events because it coincided with coverage of the royal wedding of Prince Harry and Meghan Markle, an event that caused many networks to send their staff overseas and scramble to cover the shooting back at home. The total number of sample units then was 325 across all six events. Despite this limitation in varied sample units across events, this stratified random sample was seen as more representative of the actual population than other sampling methods.

Once the sample units were obtained, the sample units were coded for the units of analysis. The unit of analysis for this study is any news clip in which the broadcaster was fully visible, meaning the coder was able to see at least the journalist's mouth, two eyebrows, and upper body, since these are key body parts involved in coding nonverbal expressions. The clip of the broadcaster was included for analysis as meeting the analysis criteria if there was no break in action – that is, it did not contain editing cuts such as going to video or another reporter/source; all clips were also at least four seconds long to help the coders have context of the nonverbal cue (Van Leeuwen & Jewitt, 2001). Both live and taped elements were included. These same criteria for the units of analysis were used by Coleman and Wu's 2006 study as well.

In total, the 325 sample units produced 3,178 units of analysis for the final sample. Columbine had 311 units of analysis, Virginia Tech had 246, Sandy Hook had 833, Umpqua had 664, Parkland had 819, and Santa Fe had 299. A power analysis run through G*Power suggests a total sample size of 227 units is sufficient for the multiple regression with 11 total predictors at a .9 power. This suggests the final sample is well above the recommended sample to have sufficient power. A second power analysis was run through G*Power for an ANOVA for the IV with the largest number of groups (source with 6 groups), at .95 power, which suggested a necessary total sample size of 102. This again affirms the sample size is more than sufficient.

Coding categories

This study utilized manual coding since the categories for examination involve subjective decision making that would be difficult if not impossible to program for a computer analysis. This study identified three coders to use in the process. Two of the coders are independent of the writing of this project, one being a former journalist while the other was representative of a general audience viewer, and I was the third coder.

The coding process, during both the intercoder phase and final sample phase, was done in two parts. First, coders independently coded the units of analysis for the six nonverbal dimensions as positive, negative, and neutral, according to nonverbal definitions (see below) without the sound on. Previous research suggests linguistic communication can interfere with the accuracy of coding nonverbal behavior (Coleman & Wu, 2006), so having the coders complete this section of analysis without being able to hear what the reporter is saying is important.

After the six nonverbal dimensions were coded, the coders independently watched the same unit of analysis with the sound on in order to obtain accurate coding about all other categories, using both linguistic, visual, and nonverbal communication from the clip to inform their decisions. However, once the codes were submitted for the nonverbal behavior, coders could not change their responses once they turned on the sound. Coders were allowed to pause the video or rewind the clips to consider their responses further in an effort to reduce confusion and encourage thoughtful coding responses. This process continued for all units of analysis.

A codebook was generated that was used during the training and coding process. The entire codebook is included in the Appendix. At the end of this chapter, Table 5.1 includes descriptive statistics for each of the dependent and independent variables.

Non-variable categories. The researcher provided the coders information about each clip, including *event name* (Columbine, Virginia Tech, Sandy Hook, Umpqua, Parkland, or Sante Fe), *year of event* (determined by the date of the event), and the *time of the clip* (in Eastern, converted if necessary). In addition, the coders logged each clip for *length in seconds* based on the inclusion and exclusion requirements of the units of analysis.

Dependent variable measures. Coders evaluated the units for six nonverbal dimension factors – eyebrows, mouth and lips, head, overall face, overall body, and overall gesturing (Ekman, 1984; Knapp & Hall, 2014). These dimensions have been used in previous research (Coleman & Wu, 2006; Zimmerman, 2014), and they are visual forms of nonverbal communication seen in almost every clip of a broadcaster. The coders did not try to determine which discrete emotion the reporter showed (such as anger or sadness), in an effort to reduce coding bias. Instead, they judged movements along three dimensions – positive, negative, and neutral; this is according to standards set by nonverbal experts (Ekman, 1984; Knapp & Hall, 2014) in order to increase intercoder reliability and measurement validity.

Table 5.1 Descriptives of independent variables, with number and percent of units of analysis by category

Individual-level characteristics	n (%) (Total N = 3,177)
Age group of victims	
Youngest	1145 (36.04%)
Mid-range	1120 (35.25%)
Oldest	912 (29.71%)
Number of death (%)	
Highest	1081 (34.03%)
Mid-range	1131 (35.60%)
Lowest	965 (30.37%)
Physical proximity/location	
Scene	948 (29.84%)
Secondary scene	154 (4.85%)
Alternative scene	167 (5.26%)
Newsroom	1908 (60.05%)
Affiliations	
Local	476 (14.98%)
National	2701 (85.02%)
Stage	
One	925 (29.12%)
Two	1181 (37.17%)
Three	1071 (33.71%)
Gender	
Female	1123 (35.35%)
Male	2054 (64.65%)
Race	
White	2524 (79.45%)
Black	318 (10.01%)
Asian	124 (3.90%)
Hispanic	211 (6.64%)
Social-level factors	
Role performance	
Disseminator	946 (29.78%)
Interpretative	1457 (45.86%)
Adversarial	484 (15.23%)
Populist-mobilizer	290 (9.13%)
Framing	
Very episodic	2236 (70.38%)
Somewhat episodic	506 (15.92%)
Somewhat thematic	357 (11.24%)
Very thematic	78 (2.46%)
Topic	
Facts	1500 (47.21%)
Policy	727 (22.88%)
Reactions	597 (18.79%)
First-hand accounts	353 (11.11%)
Source	
Officials	1116 (35.13%)
Experts	393 (12.37%)
Communities	697 (21.94%)
Victims of previous events	52 (1.64%)
Journalists	246 (7.74%)
No source	673 (21.18%)

Note: N = total units of analysis; n = subsamples for independent variables.

Coders used a six-dimension pattern of nonverbal behavior, which has demonstrated validity in other studies of gesture and appearance (Ekman, 1984; Knapp & Hall, 2014). The description for each of the six nonverbal dimensions and their positive, negative, and neutral definitions is provided here:

- eyebrows
    - negative if lowered or furrowed toward middle; movement is below neutral position
    - positive if raised up or not furrowed; movement is above neutral position
    - neutral if normal or expressionless; there is no movement, eyebrows are in neutral position
- mouth and lips
    - negative if corners contracted or pulled back as if in a grimace, tight, or frowning; movement is below neutral position
    - positive if raised, or retracted and raised as if smiling laughing; movement is above neutral position
    - neutral if normal or non-expressive; there is no movement, mouth/lips are in neutral position
- head
    - negative if head turned facing downward as if dejected or tired; head is tilted below neutral position
    - positive if head or chin pointed up; head is tilted above neutral position
    - neutral if normally positioned or straightforward; there is no movement, head is in neutral position
- overall face
    - negative if serious, intense, unhappy, or worried; facial muscles are turned downward from neutral position
    - positive if happy, lighthearted, calm, or peaceful; facial muscles are turned upward from neutral position
    - neutral if normal or expressionless; there is no movement, facial muscles are in neutral position
- overall body
    - negative if stiff or tense, the speaker is leaning forward as if hunched over; the body is below the neutral position
    - positive if relaxed, the speaker is leaning backward as if open and inviting; the body is above the neutral position
    - neutral if normal or expressionless; the body is straight, not leaning, and in neutral position
- overall gesturing
    - negative if journalist engaged in a lot of gesturing, hand-waving, or so forth at shoulder level or above; hands and arms are moving below neutral position

- positive if small expressions with hands at waist level or below shoulder level; hands and arms are moving above neutral position
- neutral if none; hands and arms are not moving, they are in neutral position

These six dimensions and their positive, negative, and neutral definitions were used in previous studies (Coleman & Wu, 2006; Zimmerman, 2014; Deavours, 2020b).

Dependent variable: Nonverbal neutrality score (NNS). After the coding was complete, each of the six codes for the nonverbal dimensions was transformed according to the two dependent variables discussed in the literature review. *NNS* allows for the measure of how neutral or nonneutral the overall presentation was, but it does not account for valence of expressions. All six of the nonverbal dimension categories were recoded into new variables (e.g. Eyebrows -> NNSEyebrows). Any original code of positive or negative was recoded into a 1 for its NNS nonverbal dimension, while anything coded neutral originally was recoded as a 0 in the new NNS category.

Total *NNS* was then calculated by summing all six variables for a total score, ranging from 0, meaning all six nonverbal dimensions were neutral, to 6, meaning all six nonverbal dimensions were nonneutral (without differentiation between positive or negative). This allows the researcher to examine the degree of neutrality in the broadcaster's nonverbal expressions as a whole, and it does not factor in the valence of those expressions, nor cancel out equal representation of positive and negative codes. This method was used in previous studies (Deavours, 2020b; Zimmerman, 2014).

Dependent variable: Janis–Fadner coefficient of imbalance (JF). Each of the six codes for the original nonverbal dimensions were transformed for a second measure of nonverbal neutrality, which used the Janis–Fadner (*JF*) coefficient of imbalance. *JF* is a measure of the valence of nonverbal behavior, either positive, negative, or neutral in emotional expression. All six of the nonverbal dimension categories were recoded into new variables (e.g. Eyebrows -> JFEyebrows). Any original code of positive was recoded into +1, an original code of negative was recoded into a −1, and an original code of neutral was recoded as a 0 in the corresponding new *JF* categories. The coefficient is calculated through a statistical measure of the extent of difference in the ratios of favorable, unfavorable, or balanced/neutral expressions for each unit of analysis. *JF* ranges from +1.0, the strongest positively valenced nonverbal reaction, to −1.0, the strongest negatively valenced nonverbal reaction. *JF* scores are negatively further away from zero when the frequency of unfavorable reactions increases; *JF* scores are positively further away from zero when the frequency of favorable reactions increase. *JF* equals 0 when the dimensions are neutral, or the number of positive and negative codes are equal (Janis & Fadner, 1949).

It is important to note the valence of nonverbal behavior does not necessarily correspond to negative or positive emotion definitions; for instance, nonverbal scholars suggest that the negative emotion of anger commonly involves raising eyebrows and gesturing above the shoulders, which are positive codes (e.g. Cohen et al., 2007). This method has been used by previous scholars (Coleman & Wu, 2006).

Independent variable measures: Individual-level. As previously discussed in Chapter 4, broadcasters' nonverbal neutrality may be influenced by individual-level factors based on BET approaches. Each of the independent variables based on individual-level factors' forms of measure are described below.

Severity: Average age of victims

The average age of victims was used as an operationalization of the severity of the event. The age of victims is an ordinal-level variable that uses the categories of 1-youngest, 2-middle, or 3-oldest age group designations. These were calculated by averaging the ages of all the victims for each event, retrieved from researching the victim lists from each event. The ages of victims were averaged by event to create a mean age for each of the six events. The lowest average age was 15 (for Sandy Hook), while the highest average age was 33 (for Virginia Tech). The mean average age of victims across all six events was 22.00 ($SD = 6.47$). The average ages were then categorized into *oldest*, *middle*, and *youngest* victim age groups. Those with the 1-youngest victims were Sandy Hook and Columbine; the 2-middle age group included Parkland and Santa Fe; the 3-oldest age group of victims was Virginia Tech and Umpqua. For the multiple regression analysis, this was recoded from an ordinal into a dichotomous variable: *youngest* (Sandy Hook, Columbine, Santa Fe) and *oldest* (Parkland, Umpqua, and Virginia Tech).

Severity: Number of victims

The number of victims was used as an operationalization of the severity of the event as well. The number of deaths is an ordinal-level variable that uses the categories of 1-highest, 2-middle, or 3-least number of deaths. The fatalities for each case were collected from the Gun Violence Archives database (2020) to categorize the events. The researcher did not include the death or injury of the shooter(s), if one occurred. The 1-highest death toll group included Virginia Tech with 32 deaths and Sandy Hook with 28 deaths; the 2-middle number of deaths group included Parkland with 17 deaths and Columbine with 13 deaths; the 3-least death group included Santa Fe with 10 deaths and Umpqua with 9 deaths. The average number of deaths across all six cases was 18.00 ($SD = 6.47$) deaths. For the multiple regression analysis, this was recoded from an ordinal into a dichotomous variable: *highest* (Virginia Tech, Sandy Hook, and Parkland) and *lowest* (Columbine, Santa Fe, and Umpqua).

Proximity: Location

Proximity to the scene is the physical distance away from the crisis and those affected. Proximity was measured in four categories. The closest proximal location was 1-scene, which included the school and its staging area(s); the next closest was 2-secondary scene, which included an area in the affected community that was not the scene, such as the shooter's home, a vigil, the hospital, etc.; the next closest was 3-alternative scene, which was a location in the field that was not in the affected community, such as the White House; the least proximal scene was 4-newsroom, since journalists are more isolated than those working in the field. There was also an option for 5-undetermined, but no units were coded in this category. For the multiple regression, this was categorized from an ordinal to a dichotomous variable, as 1-*closest* (scene and secondary scene) and 2-*furthest* (alternative and newsroom).

Proximity: Affiliation

The emotional proximity, or affiliation, of the broadcaster was based on whether the reporter was working for the local or national station at the time of the report. This was determined by coders in multiple ways: using verbal cues in descriptions about the reporters (such as the anchor saying "Joe Smith with local affiliate KXYZ reporting"), the station flag on the reporter's microphone (such as having a KXYZ mic flag as opposed to CNN's), and graphics identifying the broadcaster. Coders coded journalists as 1-local, 2-national, or 3-unknown.

Proximity: Stages

Chronemic proximity is how far away in time the report is from when the initial event began. This was determined by the stage of coverage in which the report occurred, where the 1-first stage was hours 1–8, the 2-second stage was hours 9–16, and the 3-third stage was hours 17–24. Coleman and Wu (2006) used this variable in their study of the nonverbal neutrality of 9/11 coverage, based on Graber's (2002) stages of crisis coverage theory.

Gender of broadcaster

Broadcaster gender was based on visual cues of the biological sex of the broadcaster, where 1 is female, 2 is male, and 3 is undetermined. There were no undetermined units. As content analysis can only code from visible, surface-level factors, sex was assumed by coders based on physical appearance, a limitation of this study not being able to factor for those not visibly presenting the same as their sex and/or gender.

Race of broadcasters

The race of the broadcaster was based on visual cues of the perceived race or ethnicity of a broadcaster. Definitions were based on those provided in the U.S. Census (2020). The categories included 1-white; 2-Black; 3-Asian; 4-Hispanic; 5-Native Islander (inclusive of Native Hawaiian, Other Pacific Islander, American Indian, and Alaska Native categories); and 6-undetermined. As content analysis can only code from visible, surface-level factors, race was assumed by coders based on physical appearance, a limitation of this study not being able to factor for those of different or mixed races not visibly apparent to the coders.

Social-level variables: Typifications

As described in Chapter 4, broadcasters work through routines and typifications that influence their newsmaking decisions. The social-level typification factors' forms of measure are described below.

Role performance

Coders determined the role performed by the journalist during the clip. The coders were provided Weaver, Willnat, and Wilhoit's (2019) definitions of the dissemination, interpretative, adversarial, and populist-mobilizer roles, and asked to determine which role was performed by the broadcaster in the unit. These operationalizations of role performance have been used in other prior studies (Tandoc et al., 2013). The coders chose the most dominant role performed in the clip: 1-dissemination, 2-interpretive, 3-adversarial, 4-populist-mobilizer, and 5-undetermined. There were no undetermined codes. For the multiple regression analysis, the variable was recoded so the disseminator role, which most clearly aligns with the professional norms of American objective reporting, was used as the reference category, and the three other categories were dummy coded into 1 = category; 0 = other.

Framing

The coders categorized each clip as containing either episodic or thematic frames, based on the definitions from Iyengar (1991). Researchers also suggest that coverage can include both frames, looking not only at individual issues for the event but broadening that out with more thematic coverage within one report (Jha, 2007). Therefore, the coders determined the level of episodic or thematic frame through the use of a Likert-scale, where 1-entirely episodic, 2-mostly episodic with some thematic elements, 3-equal parts episodic and thematic, 4-mostly thematic with some episodic elements, and 5-entirely thematic. This measure has been used in previous research (Broussard, 2019). For the regression, this was recoded into a dichotomous variable of 1-episodic and 2-thematic.

Topic

In addition, coders determined the topic of the report after examining definitions for each topic along with examples of each. There were four categories for topic, generated from previous research categories of topics from prior crisis research (e.g. McCluskey, 2016). They included 1-facts, which included verified details about the timeline of events, the shooter, the weapons used, the investigation, and the condition of the victims; 2-policy, which included gun laws, mental health regulation, and school safety measures; 3-reactions, which included how the community was coping, national reaction to the event, and politicians' reactions or statements on the event (that did not cover policy issues); and 4-first-hand accounts, which included talking about statements or stories shared from witnesses, survivors, and victims' family members. For the multiple regression, "facts" was chosen as the reference category, since most standards of objectivity refer to an emphasis on facts. The other topic categories were dummy coded into 1 = *category* and 0 = *other*, measured against the reference category.

Source type

Source types were pulled from prior research on crisis coverage and typical school shooting information sources (e.g. McCluskey, 2016). The types of sources include 1-officials, which included law enforcement, first responders, school officials, and elected officials; 2-experts, which included legal experts, law enforcement experts (personnel not active in law enforcement for this event), mental health experts, and interest groups or lobbyists; 3-communities, including survivors, witnesses, family members of victims or the suspect, members of the community where the event occurred, or national reactions/man-on-the-street sources; 4-victim of previous event, which was any victim or person involved in a previous school shooting; 5-journalists, which included either naming another media source (such as "*The New York Times* is reporting...") or the journalist themselves presenting their own personal opinion or accounts from experience; 6-no source given, which was any time a source was not named in the report. For the regression, officials were chosen as the reference category, since journalists use sources most often. Other categories were dummy coded into 1 = category and 0 = other to be measured against the reference category.

See Table 5.1 for a list of the dependent and independent variables, as well as descriptive statistics of their means, standard deviations, and/or percentages.

Coding process

The coders conducted intercoder reliability coding. Once training on the codebook was complete, the coders independently coded 10% of the originally desired sampling units from the total population (n = 42) (Krippendorff, 2018). There was a total of 310 units of analysis represented within the 42 sample units. None of the clips that were used in intercoder reliability training were used in the final sample for the study. Once the three coders coded the intercoder sample, the researcher ran intercoder reliability analysis using RECAL3 using the Krippendorff (2018) alpha indicator; .8 and above is considered an acceptable range for Krippendorff's alpha (2018). All categories were above this range.

The 325 sample units were coded for all of the above categories. There were a total of 3,178 units of analysis that were coded for these 14 categories. Because of the cost of coders, as well as the emotional impact of the material, I coded the final sample units alone. However, additional reliability checks were conducted as the sixth step of content analysis. One of the other coders completed reliability checks on 33 units (10% of the final sample) to ensure similar responses based on the codebook; all 14 categories were met at a .8 and above Krippendorff alpha level, using RECAL2.

Chapters 6 and 7 provide the findings of the appropriate statistical analyses for the hypotheses and research questions.

References

ADL, Anti-Defamation League. (2015, October 23). Plumbing the depths: Were the Umpqua shootings an Anti-Christian hate crime? *ADL Blog.* https://www.adl.org/blog/plumbing-the-depths-were-the-umpqua-shootings-an-anti-christian-hate-crime

Althaus, S. L. (2002). American news consumption during times of national crisis. *PS: Political Science & Politics, 35*(3), 517–521.

Broussard, R. (2019). A field theory analysis of sports journalists' coverage of social justice protests in sports (Doctoral dissertation). https://search.proquest.com/openview/9b643c21accd24607fb56d553041b19e/1?pq-origsite=gscholar&cbl=18750&diss=y

Cohen, J. F., Ambadar, Z., & Ekman, P. (2007). Observer-based measurement of facial expression with the Facial Action Coding System. In J. A. Coan & J. J. B. Allen (Eds.), *Handbook of emotion elicitation and assessment.* Oxford University Press.

Coleman, R., & Wu, D. (2006, June 7). More than words alone: Incorporating broadcasters' nonverbal communication into the stages of crisis coverage theory – evidence from September 11. *Journal of Broadcasting & Electronic Media, 50*(1), 1–17.

Cullen, D. (2009). *Columbine.* Twelve.

Cullen, D. (2019). *Parkland.* RiverRun.

Deavours, D. (2020b). Written all over their faces: Bias and nonverbal expressions in Sandy Hook coverage. *Electronic News, 14*(3), 123–142.

Deutch, G. (2019, May 17). The school shooting America forgot. *The Atlantic.* https://www.theatlantic.com/education/archive/2019/05/santa-fe-texas-school-shooting-america-forgot/589552/

Ekman, P. (1984). Expression and the nature of emotion. In K. Scherer & P. Ekman (Eds.), *Approaches to emotion* (pp. 319–344). Erbaum.

Graber, D. (2002). *Mass media and American politics* (6th ed.). CQ Press.

Gun Violence Archive. (2020). School shooting incident database. https://www.gunviolencearchive.org/query/dc04d5d0-52aa-40d2-bffd-1e8c3c1bfbf8?sort=desc&order=%23%20Killed

Holsti, O. (1969). Content analysis: An introduction. In *Content analysis for the social sciences and humanities* (pp. 1–23). Addison-Wesley.

Internet Archive. (2020). https://archive.org/

Iyengar, S. (1991). The media game: New moves, old strategies. *Press, Politics, and Political Science, 9*(1), 1–6.

Janis, I. L., & Fadner, R. (1949). Coefficients of imbalance. In H. Laswell, N. Leites & Associates (Eds.), *Language of politics: Studies in quantitative semantics* (pp. 153–189). Stewart.

Jha, S. (2007). Exploring internet influence on the coverage of social protests: Content analysis comparing protest coverage in 1967 and 1999. *Journalism & Mass Communication Quarterly, 84*(1), 40–57.

Kaid, L., & Wadsworth, A. (1989). Content analysis. In P. Emmert & L. Barker (Eds.), *Measurement of communication behavior* (pp. 197–217). Longman.

Knapp, M., & Hall, J. (2014). *Nonverbal communication in human interaction* (8th ed.). Wadsworth.

Krippendorff, K. (2018). *Content analysis: An introduction to its methodology* (4th ed.). Sage.

Maddox, B. (2007, April 20). Why NBC was right to show those demented ramblings. *The Times*. Archived from the original on April 29, 2011.

McCluskey, M. (2016). *News framing of school shootings: Journalism and American social problems*. Lexington Books.

Neuendorf, K. (2002). Defining content analysis. In K. Krippendorff (Ed.), *The content analysis guidebook* (pp. 1–25). Sage Publications.

Tandoc, E. C., Hellmueller, L., & Vos, T. P. (2013). Mind the gap: Between journalistic role conception and enactment. *Journalism Practice, 7*(5), 539–554.

U.S. Census Bureau. (2020). Population. https://www.census.gov/topics/population.html

Van Leeuwen, T., & Jewitt, C. (2001). *Handbook of visual analysis*. Sage.

Weaver, D., Willnat, L., & Wilhoit, G. (2019). The American journalist in the digital age: Another look at U.S. news people. *Journalism & Mass Communication Quarterly, 96*(1), 101–130.

Xigen, L., Lindsay, L., Mogensen, K. (2002). Media in a crisis situation involving national interest: A content analysis of the TV networks coverage of the 9/11 incident during the first eight hours. Paper presented at AEJMC 2002, Miami Beach, FL. http://aejmc.org/_events/convention/abstracts/2002/rtvj.php

Zimmerman, J. (2014). Media bias through facial expressions on local Las Vegas television news programs: A visual content analysis [master's thesis]. University of Nevada, Las Vegas.

6 Predictive influences on nonverbal neutrality

Findings

This study utilizes content analysis in order to examine the variability of the nonverbal neutrality of broadcasters during crisis coverage, exploring individual- and social-level influences as well as their interactions. This chapter will present the key findings from this analysis in order to further develop theory predicting the influences on journalists' nonverbal neutrality during crises.

Overall nonverbal neutrality

The results suggest that broadcasters were more nonneutral than neutral in their nonverbal behaviors. Of 3,177 units of analysis, the average nonverbal neutrality score (*NNS*) was 3.31 (*SD* = 1.68) across the six dimensions. A higher score indicates less neutrality; so, on average, journalists showed slightly more nonneutral than neutral expressions.

The average *Janis–Fadner coefficient* (*JF*) was –.06 (*SD* = .22). The *JF* is scaled –1 (negative) to 1 (positive), and so on average, broadcasters were more likely to have moderately strong negative valence in nonverbal behaviors. This indicates unfavorable valences during the coverage, such as displaying nonverbal expressions related to anger, sadness, fear, disgust, or contempt. These results are particularly important as broadcasters report wanting a standard of complete nonverbal neutrality (which would be represented by an *NNS* and *JF* of 0) while discussing nonverbal's normative boundaries (Deavours, 2022).

The event with the lowest *NNS*, or most neutral nonverbal expressions, was Virginia Tech, while Parkland had the highest *NNS*, or least neutral expressions. For *JF*, Virginia Tech had the closest score to zero, and thus the most neutral nonverbal valence, and Santa Fe had the furthest *JF* from zero, or the most negatively valenced nonverbal behavior. See Table 6.1.

H1: Age of victims

To test H1, which stated the younger the age group of the victims in the event, the less neutral the nonverbal behavior of journalists will be, a one-way ANOVA was conducted. ANOVA assumptions were assessed. One-way

DOI: 10.4324/9781003375340-6

Table 6.1 Descriptive statistics: Means and standard deviations for NNS and JF by event

	Total (N = 3,177)	Columbine (N = 311)	Virginia Tech (N = 247)	Sandy Hook (N = 834)	Umpqua (N = 665)	Parkland (N = 820)	Santa Fe (N = 300)
NNS	3.31 (1.68)	2.72 (1.61)	2.57 (1.61)	3.34 (1.74)	3.37 (1.55)	3.64 (1.62)	3.47 (1.71)
JF	-.06 (.22)	-.06 (.18)	-.02 (.14)	-.08 (.25)	-.05 (.17)	-.05 (.25)	-.10 (.24)

Table 6.2 H1: ANOVA results for nonverbal neutrality and age of shooting victims

Dependent variables	Youngest victims M(SD)	Mid-age victims M(SD)	Oldest victims M(SD)	Welch's F	d.f.
NNS	3.17(1.73)	3.59(1.65)	3.15(1.61)	24.681*	2, 2080.21
JF	−.07(.23)	−.06(.25)	−.04(.17)	8.615*	2, 2110.91

Note: significance indicated by * $p < .001$.

ANOVAs were conducted to compare the nonverbal neutrality of broadcasters relative to the age groups of victims, for both *JF* and *NNS* variables. See Table 6.2.

H1 was not supported for the test of *NNS* because, while results were significant, they did not follow the expected pattern: journalists were less nonverbally neutral when covering midrange age groups compared to younger groups. Therefore, evidence for *NNS* is not consistent with the BET-based expectation that journalists will appear less neutral when they cover younger victims.

Looking at the statistics, Welch's ANOVA results show a significant difference in the nonverbal neutrality of broadcasters by age of victims, both for *NNS* [Welch's $F(2, 2080.21) = 24.68$, $p < .005$, partial $\eta2 = .02$] and *JF* [Welch's $F(2, 2110.91) = 8.62$, $p < .005$, partial $\eta2 = .004$]. There was an increase in the mean *NNS* (meaning broadcasters became less neutral) from the *oldest* ($M = 3.15$, $SD = 1.61$) to *youngest* ($M = 3.17$, $SD = 1.73$) to *middle* ($M = 3.59$; $SD = 1.65$) age groups, in that order.

H1 is supported using *JF* since there is a significant and more negative nonverbal reaction for broadcasters reporting on cases with younger children compared to cases with middle and older age victims. Since *JF* is a measure of emotional valence, this suggests broadcasters are emotionally reacting to the severity factor of age of victims, consistent with a BET perspective.

Looking at the statistics, *JF* was progressively further away from zero (meaning more negatively valenced) from *oldest* ($M = -.04$, $SD = .17$), to *middle* ($M = -.06$, $SD = .25$), to *youngest* ($M = -.07$, $SD = .23$) age groups.

Overall, both *NNS* and *JF* vary significantly based on the age of victims, but the hypothesized difference direction held only for *JF*. This aligns with BET, which suggests journalists' nonverbal reaction would be most negative when covering younger victims, a more severe and disturbing crisis. It is also notable that age is the only individual-level variable that is significant for *JF*.

NNS, a measure only of the journalist's expression neutrality and less sensitive to emotional valence, was not as affected by crisis severity in terms of victims' age. This suggests the age of victims may not change the journalists'

Table 6.3 H2: ANOVA for nonverbal neutrality and number of deaths in shooting

Dependent variables	Highest death rate M(SD)	Middle death rate M(SD)	Lowest death rate M(SD)	Welch's F	d.f.
NNS	3.16(1.74)	3.38(1.67)	3.40(1.60)	6.70*	2, 2102.02
JF	−.07(.23)	−.05(.23)	−.06(.20)	1.13	2, 2113.98

Note: significance indicated by * $p < .05$.

norms of display; for instance, journalists may normatively consider all deaths to need the same nonverbal display regardless of age.

H2: Number of shooting victims

H2 states that the more deaths during the shooting, the less neutral the nonverbal behavior of broadcast journalists will be following the shooting. Results are in Table 6.3.

H2 is not supported using *NNS* since the BET-based predicted direction of neutrality variance was not found. Instead of highest deaths being the least neutral, they were the most neutral, and those with the lowest deaths were the least neutral. H2 is also not supported for *JF* since it was not statistically significant.

Looking at the data, Welch's ANOVA results show there was a significant difference in the nonverbal neutrality of broadcasters by deaths for *NNS* [Welch's $F(2, 2102.02) = 6.70$, $p = .001$, partial $\eta2 = .004$], but not for *JF* [Welch's $F(2, 2113.98) = 1.13$, $p = .33$]. There was an increase in mean *NNS* (meaning less neutral) from the *highest* number of deaths $(M = 3.16, SD = .05)$, to the *middle* $(M = 3.38, SD = .05)$, to the *lowest* $(M = 3.40, SD = .05)$. This indicates that the higher the death toll of an event, the more likely it was that journalists would be nonverbally neutral.

While *NNS* was significant, it was the events with the lowest death rate that had the least neutral nonverbal behavior. This may be explained by coping mechanisms of vicarious traumatization that require working in overwhelming trauma to compartmentalize more and work by more strict standards of professional practice due to the increased severity (Collins & Long, 2003); previous studies with journalists have found journalists tend to disassociate from trauma around them (Deavours, 2022), which may be factoring into their nonverbal displays as well.

H3: Physical proximity to shooting

To examine H3, which states that the closer a journalist is physically to the location of the crisis scene when reporting, the less neutral their nonverbal

Table 6.4 H3: ANOVA for nonverbal neutrality and physical proximity to scene of shooting

Dependent variables	Scene of shooting M(SD)	Secondary scene M(SD)	Alternative scene M(SD)	Newsroom M(SD)	F	d.f.
NNS	3.21(1.65)	3.36(1.60)	3.34(1.47)	3.36(1.71)	(Welch's) 1.66	3, 427.62
JF	−.07(.21)	−.07(.22)	−.04(.19)	−.06(.23)	1.58	3, 153

behavior will be, a one-way ANOVA was conducted. A Welch's ANOVA was used for *NNS* since Levene's test was significant, but the test was not significant for *JF* ($p = .63$), so a standard ANOVA was conducted. See Table 6.4.

H3 is not supported since physical proximity was not significant in terms of varying broadcasters' nonverbal behavior, regardless of whether measuring by movement (*NNS*) or valence (*JF*). Results show no significant difference for *NNS* [Welch's $F(3, 427.62) = 1.66$, $p = .18$], or *JF* [$F (3, 153) = 1.58$, $p = .19$].

Despite BET suggesting nonverbal behavior would vary based on how close the broadcaster is to the trauma, there was neither a large nor significant difference in nonverbal neutrality from journalists in different locations. H3 is not supported.

H4: Affiliation: Local or national broadcasters

To test H4, which predicts local journalists will be less neutral in their nonverbal behaviors than national journalists, an independent-sample t-test was conducted.

H4 is not supported for *NNS* or *JF* since neither shows a significant difference. There was not a significant difference in *NNS* for *local* broadcasters ($M = 3.31$, $SD = 1.46$) and *national* broadcasters ($M = 3.32$, $SD = 1.71$), $M = −.01$, 95% CI [−.16, .14], $t(725.39) = −.11$, $p = .91$. There was also not a significant difference in *JF* between *local* broadcasters ($M = −.06$, $SD = .20$) and *national* broadcasters ($M = −.05$, $SD = .22$), $M = −.002$, 95% CI [−.02, .02], $t(691.45) = −.16$, $p = .87$.

These findings suggest broadcasters do not differ in nonverbal neutrality by affiliation. While BET suggests local journalists who are more emotionally connected to the affected communities would be less neutral in their reaction to stimuli, there was not a large or significant difference between the nonverbal neutrality of local and national journalists. This may suggest widely held standards of reporting practice regardless of the communities and audiences served.

Table 6.5 H5: ANOVA for nonverbal neutrality and chronemic proximity

Dependent variables	1st stage M(SD)	2nd stage M(SD)	3rd stage M(SD)	Welch's F	d.f.
NNS	3.14(1.72)	3.23(1.59)	3.55(1.70)	17.00*	2, 2047.85
JF	−.06(.21)	−.06(.20)	−.06(.25)	.269	2, 2033.45

Note: significance indicated by * $p < .001$.

H5: Graber's stages of coverage

H5 predicted the nonverbal behavior of broadcast journalists will follow an inverted U pattern, where broadcasters at the beginning and end of the event will present more neutral nonverbal behaviors than those in the middle of the event. Results are reported in Table 6.5.

H5 is not supported using *NNS* since the predicted direction of neutrality variance was not found. According to Graber's (2002) research on reporting during crisis, broadcasters should be midrange in neutrality in stage one, the least neutral in stage two, and the most neutral in stage three; that pattern was not seen. Instead, *NNS* showed broadcasters got progressively less neutral as coverage shifted from stage one to stage three. H5 is also not supported by *JF* since differences across the three stages were not significant.

Looking at the data, Welch's ANOVA results show there was a significant difference in the nonverbal neutrality of broadcasters by chronemic proximity for the *NNS* [Welch's $F(2, 2047.85) = 17.00$, $p < .001$, partial $\eta2 = .01$], but not for *JF* [Welch's $F(2, 2033.45) = .27$, $p = .76$]. There was an increase in mean *NNS* from the *first* ($M = 3.14$, $SD = 1.72$), to the *second* ($M = 3.23$, $SD = 1.59$), to the *third* ($M = 3.55$, $SD = 1.70$) stages.

This suggests that, the further in time from the event that the broadcasters' report was, the less neutral their presentations were. This suggests the 24-hour time limit may be preventing researchers from seeing when journalists eventually return to neutrality standards during event coverage, if they do at all.

H6: Gender of journalist

To examine H6, which states female journalists will be less neutral in their nonverbal behaviors than male journalists, an independent-samples t-test was conducted.

H6 is supported for *NNS* since female broadcasters showed less neutral nonverbal behaviors than males. *NNS* was significantly different between *female* ($M = 3.43$, $SD = 1.63$) and *male* ($M = 3.25$, $SD = 1.70$) broadcasters, $M = .18$, 95% CI [.06, .30], $t(2392.75) = 3.00$, $p = .003$.

H6 is not supported for *JF*, though, since it was not significant. There was not a significant difference in *JF* between *female* ($M = -.06$, $SD = .23$) and *male* ($M = -.06$, $SD = .22$) broadcasters, $M = .002$, 95% CI [$-.01$, $.02$], $t(2197.41) = .26$, $p = .80$.

In sum, H6 is only supported for *NNS*, but not *JF*. Female broadcasters are more likely to demonstrate nonneutral nonverbal behaviors compared to male broadcasters, which is consistent with previous research that women tend to be more expressive than males. However, the overall emotionality of broadcasters' nonverbal neutrality (*JF*) does not vary by gender, meaning both genders are similar in their negative valence of coverage. This suggests journalists may have different social expectations for display dependent on cultural expectations of gender, while there is not as much difference in emotionality displays by gender.

H7: Race of journalist

To examine H7, which states nonverbal behavior will vary significantly based on the race of the journalist, an ANOVA was conducted. Results are reported in Table 6.6.

H7 is supported for *NNS* since race was significant, where Black journalists were the most neutral and Asian journalists were the least neutral. H7 is not supported for *JF* since it was not statistically significant.

Looking at the statistics, Welch's ANOVA results show there was a significant difference in the nonverbal neutrality of broadcasters by journalists' race for the *NNS* [Welch's $F(3, 356.42) = 4.37$, $p = .01$, partial $\eta2 = .004$], but not for *JF* [Welch's $F(3, 370.17) = 2.22$, $p = .09$]. There was an increase in mean *NNS* (meaning less neutral) from *Black* ($M = 3.15$, $SD = 1.70$), to *white* ($M = 3.30$, $SD = 1.69$), to *Hispanic* ($M = 3.57$, $SD = 1.47$), to *Asian* ($M = 3.59$, $SD = 1.59$).

In sum, findings suggest there is no difference in emotionality of reaction during the events between races, but overall nonverbal neutrality is affected by the race of the broadcaster. This suggests journalists may have different social expectations for display dependent on cultural expectations of race, while there is not as much difference in emotionality displays by race.

Table 6.6 H7: ANOVA for nonverbal neutrality and journalist race

Dependent variables	Black M(SD)	White M(SD)	Hispanic M(SD)	Hispanic M(SD)	Welch's F	d.f.
NNS	3.15 (1.70)	3.30(1.69)	3.57(1.47)	3.59(1.45)	4.37*	3, 356.42
JF	−.04(.17)	−.06(.23)	−.06(.16)	−.07(.22)	2.22	3, 370.17

Note: significance indicated by * $p = .01$.

Table 6.7 H8: ANOVA for nonverbal neutrality and journalist role performance

DV	Disseminator M(SD)	Interpretative M(SD)	Populist-mobilizer M(SD)	Adversarial M(SD))	Welch's F	d.f.
NNS	2.64(1.60)	3.27(1.56)	3.52(1.56)	4.65(1.42)	200.36*	3, 997.96
JF	−.03(.16)	−.05(.22)	−.07(.22)	−.13(.30)	14.95*	3, 940.29

Note: significance indicated by * $p < .001$.

H8: Journalistic role performance

H8 states there will be a significant difference between the neutrality of journalists' behavior when performing different roles. Additionally, H8a predicts broadcasters performing disseminator roles will be the most neutral, while H8b predicts those performing an adversarial role will be the least neutral nonverbally. Results are reported in Table 6.7.

Findings indicate support for H8, H8a, and H8b, for *NNS*. Journalists performing the role of disseminator were most likely to show nonverbal neutrality, while those performing an adversarial or "watchdog" role were least likely to show nonverbal neutrality. Looking more closely at the data, Welch's ANOVA results show there was a significant difference in the nonverbal neutrality of broadcasters by journalists' *role* performance for *NNS* [Welch's $F(3, 997.96) = 200.36$, $p < .001$, partial $\eta2 = .15$], and *JF* [Welch's $F(3, 940.29) = 14.95$, $p < .001$, partial $\eta2 = .02$]. There was an increase in mean *NNS* (meaning it becomes less neutral) from the *disseminator* role $(M = 2.64, SD = 1.60)$, to *interpretive* $(M = 3.27, SD = 1.56)$, to *populist-mobilizer* $(M = 3.52, SD = 1.68)$, to *adversarial* $(M = 4.65, SD = 1.42)$.

H8 is also supported for *JF*, as are H8a and H8b. These findings indicate journalists performing a disseminator role are most likely to show neutrality, while those performing an adversarial role are most likely to display negatively valenced emotions like sadness, anger, fear, and disgust. Looking at the statistics, the mean *JF* progressed further from zero, and thus more negatively valenced, from *disseminator* $(M = -.03, SD = .16)$, to *interpretative* $(M = -.05, SD = .22)$, to *populist-mobilizer* $(M = -.07, SD = .22)$, to *adversarial* $(M = -.13, SD = .30)$ role performance groups.

Results are consistent across *NNS* and *JF*, which is the first finding with similar results. For both *NNS* and *JF*, journalists appear more neutral when playing the more passive disseminator role and less neutral when playing an adversarial or "watchdog" role. These findings are consistent with BECV predictions that social situations shape nonverbal behavior, both in terms of appropriate nonverbal and emotionality displays.

Table 6.8 H9: ANOVA for nonverbal neutrality and journalist framing

DV	Very episodic M(SD)	Somewhat episodic M(SD)	Somewhat thematic M(SD)	Very thematic M(SD)	Welch's F	d.f.
NNS	3.00(1.63)	3.96(1.49)	3.97(1.61)	4.95(1.43)	111.69*	3, 316.53
JF	−.05(.20)	−.07(.24)	−.09(.24)	−.21(.41)	8.32*	3, 298.09

Note: significance indicated by * $p < .001$.

H9: Episodic vs. thematic framing of shooting event

To test H9, which states journalists framing information episodically will display more nonneutral nonverbal behavior than journalists framing information thematically, an ANOVA was conducted. See Table 6.8.

H9 was supported for *NNS*: journalists were most likely to appear neutral when the event was framed episodically (focused specifically on the event), and they were least likely to appear neutral when the event was framed thematically (focused on broader issues). Looking at the statistics, Welch's ANOVA results show there was a significant difference in the nonverbal neutrality of broadcasters by journalists' framing for *NNS* [$F(3, 316.53) = 111.69$, $p < .001$, partial $\eta2 = .09$], and *JF* [Welch's $F(3, 298.90) = 8.32$, $p < .001$, partial $\eta2 = .02$]. Journalists became less neutral (meaning an increase in mean *NNS*) as framing became more thematic: from *very episodic (M* = 3.00, *SD =* 1.63), to *somewhat episodic* (*M* = 3.96, *SD* = 1.49), to *somewhat thematic* (*M* = 3.97, *SD* = 1.61), to *very thematic* (*M* = 4.95, *SD* = 1.43).

H9 was supported for *JF*. Like *NNS*, coverage became less neutral, and more negatively valenced, as the framing of the shooting event became more thematic and less focused on the facts of the specific event. Looking at the statistics, the mean *JF* progressed further from zero, and thus became more negatively valenced, from *very episodic* (*M* = −.05, *SD* = .20), to *somewhat episodic* (*M* = −.07, *SD* = .24), to *somewhat thematic* (*M* = −.09, *SD* = .24), to *very thematic* (*M* = −.21, *SD* = .41).

This suggests the more episodic the framing of the event, the more neutral the nonverbal behavior will be, regardless of whether measuring muscle movements or valence; alternatively, the more thematic the framing of the event, the less likely the nonverbal behavior will be neutral and the more unfavorable the reactions. Findings are consistent with BECV approaches for social and professional norms causing variations in nonverbal behavior and emotionality.

RQ1: Topics of news coverage

RQ1 asks whether topics of coverage predict the neutrality of nonverbal behavior of the journalist. To answer RQ1, a one-way ANOVA was conducted. Results are in Table 6.9.

Table 6.9 RQ1: ANOVA for nonverbal neutrality and topics of coverage

Dependent variables	Facts of shooting M(SD)	Reactions to shooting M(SD)	First-hand accounts M(SD)	Policy M(SD)	Welch's F	d.f.
NNS	2.95(1.66)	3.23(1.53)	3.35(1.65)	4.11(1.57)	85.90*	3, 1156.97
JF	−.04(.19)	−.05(.19)	−.07(.27)	−.10(.26)	8.703*	3, 1079.09

Note: significance indicated by * $p < .001$.

Findings for *NNS* indicate broadcasters are least neutral nonverbally when covering policy topics, but their nonverbal behaviors are most neutral when covering facts about the event. Looking at the data, Welch's ANOVA results show there was a significant difference in the nonverbal neutrality of broadcasters by topic, both for *NNS* [Welch's $F(3, 1156.97) = 85.90$, $p < .001$, partial $\eta 2 = .07$] and *JF* [Welch's $F(3, 1079.09) = 8.70$, $p < .001$, partial $\eta 2 = .01$]. There was an increase in mean *NNS* from the *facts* topic group ($M = 2.95$, $SD = 1.67$) to *reactions* ($M = 3.23$, $SD = 1.53$) to *first-hand accounts* ($M = 3.35$; $SD = 1.65$) to *policy* ($M = 4.11$, $SD = 1.57$). *Facts* were the most neutral, and *policy* was the least neutral nonverbally.

JF results show that broadcasters are most neutral when discussing facts about the event, but they are least neutral and most unfavorable when discussing policy, similar to *NNS* findings. This indicates journalists discussing policy issues are most likely to display negative emotions of fear, anger, sadness, or disgust. Mean *JF* progressed further from zero (became more negatively valenced) from *facts* ($M = -.04$, $SD = .19$), to *reactions* ($M = -.05$, $SD = .19$), to *first-hand accounts* ($M = -.07$, $SD = .27$), to *policy* ($M = -.10$, $SD = .26$).

The findings indicate the topic of coverage influences nonverbal neutrality, both in terms of movement and emotionality. As broadcasters discuss various aspects of the event, they are more likely to remain neutral when sticking to the facts, while their nonverbal neutrality decreases when discussing policy. This is consistent with BECV, as the social context shapes nonverbal behavior. It is also consistent with framing findings from H9 that journalists discussing issues that go beyond the specific facts tend to appear less neutral nonverbally.

RQ2: Sources of information

RQ2 asks whether the source affects the neutrality of nonverbal behavior of the journalist. An ANOVA was conducted to assess RQ2. Results are in Table 6.10.

RQ2 findings suggest broadcasters' nonverbal behaviors in terms of *NNS* differ based on source; the most neutral presentations involved no sources,

Table 6.10 RQ2: ANOVA for nonverbal neutrality and sources

DV	No source M(SD)	Officials M(SD)	Communities M(SD)	Previous victims M(SD)	Experts M(SD)	Journalists M(SD)	F	d.f.
NNS	2.77 (1.67)	3.14 (1.63)	3.37(1.57)	3.81(1.44)	3.88 (1.64)	4.41 (1.52)	51.04*	5, 3171
JF	−.05 (.18)	−.04(.18)	−.05(.25)	−.06(.26)	−.09 (.27)	−.13 (.27)	Welch's 6.96*	5, 428.17

Note: significance indicated by * $p < .001$.

while the least neutral presentations involved journalists as sources, such as citing themselves as a first-person witness or other media outlets. Notably, neutrality also tends to be higher when officials serve as sources and lower when experts serve as sources. ANOVA results show there was a significant difference in the nonverbal neutrality of broadcasters by source, both for the *NNS* [$F(5, 3171) = 51.04$, $p < .001$, partial $\eta2 = .07$] and *JF* [Welch's $F (5, 442.12) = 52.50$, $p < .001$, partial $\eta2 = .02$]. There was an increase in mean *NNS* (meaning less neutral) from *no source* ($M = 2.77$, $SD = 1.67$), to *officials* ($M = 3.14$, $SD = 1.62$), to *communities* ($M = 3.37$, $SD = 1.57$), to *previous victims* ($M = 3.81$, $SD = 1.44$), to *experts* ($M = 3.88$, $SD = 1.63$), to *journalists* ($M = 4.41$, $SD = 1.52$) source groups.

Tukey's post hoc analysis shows the mean difference from *officials* to *experts* (.74, 95% CI [.47, 1.01]) was significant ($p < .001$), as well as the increase from *communities* to *experts* (.51, 95% CI [.22, .80], $p < .001$), *experts* to *journalists* (.53, 95% CI [.15, .90]), $p = .001$), *no source* to *experts* (1.11, 95% CI [.82, 1.40], $p < .001$), *communities* to *officials* (.22, 95% CI [.00, .45], $p = .049$), *communities* to *journalists* (1.04, 95% CI [.70, 1.38], $p < .001$), *no source* to *communities* (.60, 95% CI [.82, 1.40], $p < .001$), *previous victims* to *officials* (.66, 95% CI [.01, 1.32], $p = .04$), *no source* to *previous victims* (1.04, 95% CI (.37, 1.70), $p < .001$), *officials* to *journalists* (.37, 95% CI [.15, .60], $p < .001$), and *no source* to *journalists* (1.64, 95% CI [.37, 1.70], $p < .001$). No other group differences were significant.

For the *JF* analysis, nonverbal neutrality differed based on source of information, with the most nonverbally neutral reports being sourced to officials or when no source is cited, and the most negative nonverbal expressions when sourcing other journalists or themselves. Looking at the statistics, there was an increase in mean *JF* (meaning more negatively valenced) from *official* ($M = -.04$, $SD = .18$) to *no source* ($M = -.05$, $SD = .18$), *communities* ($M = -.05$, $SD = .25$), *previous victim* ($M = -.06$, $SD = .26$), *experts* ($M = -.09$, $SD = .27$), and *journalists* ($M = -.13$, $SD = .27$).

Overall, findings suggest the routine practice of sourcing officials contributes to more neutral presentations of nonverbal behavior during crises, although citing no source was the most neutral for *NNS*. It is also interesting to note that broadcasters who source and talk to those most affected by the trauma, *communities*, were more neutral nonverbally than those journalists sourcing experts and journalists. These findings are generally consistent with BECV, which suggests norms of communication will change based on social interactions and expectations of groups.

RQ3: Assessing the relative importance of factors influencing neutrality (multiple regression)

RQ3 asks which factors among the individual and social levels are most important in understanding the variability of journalists' nonverbal neutrality.

A hierarchical multiple regression was conducted for both *NNS* and *JF*. Hierarchical multiple regressions allow the prediction of a dependent variable based on multiple independent variables, entering the IVs into the equation in an order of theoretical importance. This allows for control of the effects of any covariates, as well as assessing causal effects of IVs when predicting the DV.

Independent variables at the ordinal or nominal level were recoded as dummy variables as described in Chapter 5.

The full model of demographic, individual-level, stage, and typification-level characteristics to predict *NNS* (Model 4) was significant, $F(22, 3154)$ = 35.73, $p < .001$; adjusted R^2 of .20. Blocks of variables were entered. Typification variables have the strongest influence on the nonverbal neutrality of journalists, followed by individual-level factors, and then stages of coverage. Specifically, the addition of the typification factors to the prediction of *NNS* (Model 4) led to a statistically significant increase in R^2 of .19, $F(12, 3154)$ = 52.53, $p < .001$. The addition of stage of coverage factors to the prediction of *NNS* (Model 3) led to a significant increase in R^2 of .04, $F(2, 3166)$ = 18.61, $p < .001$. The addition of individual-level factors to predict *NNS* (Model 2) also led to a significant increase in R^2 of .03, $F(3, 3168)$ = 24.66, $p < .001$.

Table 6.10 reports the unstandardized (*B*) and standardized (β) regression coefficients for individual predictors in the four models, using *NNS* as the dependent variable. When the typification factors are added in the fourth model, 13 factors explained additional variance in *NNS*. Of those, role performance, specifically the *adversarial* role, explained the largest portion with a moderately strong effect ($\beta = .33$, $p < .001$), such that broadcasters performing *adversarial* roles were much less neutral (higher *NNS*) than those performing *disseminator* roles. Similarly, broadcasters performing *interpretative* roles ($\beta = .14$, $p < .001$) and those performing *populist-mobilizer* roles ($\beta = .14$, $p < .001$) are predicted to be less neutral than those performing *disseminator* roles, which suggests journalists performing the *disseminator* role are the most neutral nonverbally.

Three source categories significantly explained variance in *NNS*: *expert* ($\beta = .04$, $p < .05$), *no source* ($\beta = -.07$, $p < .001$), and *journalist* ($\beta = .13$, $p < .001$). This suggests broadcasters who use *no source* will display more neutral nonverbal behavior than those using *officials* as sources. Alternatively, those using *experts* and *journalists* as sources will display less neutral nonverbal behavior than will journalists using *official* sources. Therefore, the strongest factors in the model – role performance and source – are typification factors, suggesting more consistency with BECV-related variables.

However, two individual-level variables, *age of victims* and *number of deaths*, were still significant when stages of coverage and typification-level factors were added to the model. This suggests these factors, which are conceptually linked to individual reactions to traumatic stimuli (consistent with the BET approach), continue to hold predictive importance even when controlling for all other factors. The *age of victims* factor shows less neutral coverage for events with *younger* victims compared to *older* victims, which is consistent with BET predictions; these findings differ from those found in the one-way ANOVA in H1, which is likely caused by having to dichotomize the variable into younger and older, rather than three distinctions of age.

Affiliation did not follow the predicted BET pattern, since national broadcasters, who are less emotionally connected to the communities affected, were less neutral than local broadcasters.

It's worth noting that in the full model, race, particularly for *Black* and *Hispanic* journalists, and gender (females less neutral than males) continued to be significant even when controlling for all other factors. This suggests these demographic factors have predictive importance in terms of nonverbal neutrality. Additionally, it is important to note the regression did not find significance for stages of coverage, providing no support here for Graber's stages of crisis coverage theory (2002) (Table).

For *JF*, the full model of demographic, individual-level, stages, and typification-level characteristics to predict *JF* (Model 4) was significant, $F(22, 3154) = 5.15, p < .001$; adjusted R^2 of .03. Blocks of variables were entered. Typification-level factors have the strongest influence on the negative nonverbal reaction of journalists, compared to individual-level and stage factors, which did not significantly predict variation in the negative reactions of broadcast journalists. Specifically, the addition of typification-level factors to the prediction of *JF* (Model 4) led to a significant increase in R^2 of .04, $F(12, 3154) = 8.61, p < .001$. However, the addition of individual-level factors (Model 2) did not lead to a significant increase in R^2, $F(3, 3168) = 1.33, p = .26$, and the addition of the stage factor (Model 3) did not lead to a statistically significant increase in R^2 either, $F(2, 3166) = .50, p = .61$. Table 6.12 reports the unstandardized (*B*) and standardized (β) regression coefficients for the four models using *JF* as the dependent variable.

When typification-level factors were added in Model 4, *race=Black* (β = .04, $p < .05$) was significant, along with four others: *role = adversarial* (β = −.13, $p < .001$); *journalist as a source* (β = −.08, $p < .001$); *expert source* (β = −.04, $p < .05$); and *location* (β = .06, $p < .01$). *Adversarial* role enactment explained the largest amount of variance but still with a relatively weak effect, where broadcasters performing an *adversarial* role had a more negative *JF*, and thus more negative nonverbal reaction, than broadcasters performing a *disseminator* role. Broadcasters who used *journalists* or *experts* as sources also had a weak effect on *JF* variance, where those reporting with *journalists* or *experts* as sources were more likely to have a negative *JF*, and thus be more emotionally negative in their nonverbal reactions, than those using *officials* as sources. These findings suggest typification influences of role performance and source are the strongest predictors of emotional valence of nonverbal reactions, which shows greater consistency with BECV. These findings are similar to those of *NNS*, above.

Table 6.11 RQ3: Hierarchical multiple regression for NNS

	Model 1		Model 2		Model 3		Model 4	
	B	β	B	β	B	β	B	β
Constant	3.46***		4.67***		4.40***		4.29***	
Gender (0-female; 1-male)	-.16*	-.04*	-.10	-.03	-.07	-.02	-.12*	-.03*
Race, Black (0-white; 1-Black)	-.15	-.03	-.24*	-.04*	-.23*	-.04*	-.21*	-.04*
Race, Asian (0-white; 1-Asian)	.25	.03	.23	.03	.25	.03	.22	.03
Race, Hispanic (0-white; 1-Hispanic)	.22	.03	.20	.03	.18	.03	.35**	.05**
Affiliation (0-local; 1-national)	.06	.01	-.001	.00	-.01	-.02	-.21**	0.04**
Age of victims (0-younger; 1-older)			-.77***	-.14***	-.77***	-.14***	-.60***	-.11***
Deaths (0-lower; 1-higher)			-.35***	-.10***	-.37***	-.11***	-.30***	-.09***
Location (0-closer; 1-further)			.08	.02	.11	.03	-.03	-.01
Stage, Two (0-stage 1; 1-Stage 2)					.15*	.04*	-.07	-.02
Stage, Three (0-stage 1; 1-stage 3)					.44***	.13***	.10	.03
Frame (0-episodically; 1-thematically)							.07	.01

(Continued)

Table 6.11 (Continued)

	Model 1		Model 2		Model 3		Model 4	
	B	β	B	β	B	β	B	β
Role, interpretative (0-disseminator; 1-interpretative)							.46***	.14***
Role, adversarial (0-disseminator; 1-adversarial)							1.54***	.33***
Role, populist-mobilizer (0-disseminator; 1-populist-mobilizer)							.74***	.13***
Topic, policy (0-facts; 1-policy)							.21*	.05*
Topic, reaction (0-facts; 1-reaction)							−.10	−.02
Topic, first-hand account (0-facts; 1-first-hand acct)							.08	.02
Source, expert (0-official; 1-expert)							.22*	.04*
Source, community (0-official; 1-community)							.15	.04
Source, previous victim (0-official; 1-prev. victim)							.19	.01
Source, journalist (0-official; 1-journalist)							.80***	.13***
Source, none (0-official; 1-no source)							−.28***	−.07***

Note: $R^2 = .20$ ($p > .001$); B – unstandardized coefficient beta; β – standardized coefficients beta; N = 3,177;
*$p < .05$; **$p < .01$; ***$p < .001$.
Note: negative coefficients = less neutrality.

Table 6.12 RQ3: Hierarchical multiple regression for JF

	Model 1		Model 2		Model 3		Model 4	
	B	β	B	β	B	β	B	β
Constant	-.06**		-.09*		-.09*		-.07	
Gender (0-female; 1-male)	-.003	-.01	-.003	-.01	-.004	-.01	.001	.001
Race, Black (0-white; 1-Black)	.03*	.04*	.03	.04	.03	.04	.03*	.04*
Race, Asian (0-white; 1-Asian)	-.002	-.002	.001	.001	.001	.001	.002	.002
Race, Hispanic (0-white; 1-Hispanic)	-.004	-.004	-.001	-.001	-.001	-.001	-.01	-.01
Affiliation (0-local; 1-national)	.004	.01	.003	.01	.003	.01	.01	.02
Age of victims (0-younger; 1-older)			.01	.01	.01	.01	-.01	-.01
Deaths (0-lower; 1-higher)			-.01	-.01	-.01	-.02	-.01	-.03
Location (0-closer; 1-further)			.02	.03	.02	.03	.03**	.06**
Stage, two (0-stage 1; 1-stage 2)					.01	.02	.02	.04
Stage, three (0-stage 1; 1-stage 3)					-.002	-.004	.02	.03
Frame (0-episodically; 1-thematically)							-.02	-.03

(*Continued*)

Table 6.12 (Continued)

	Model 1		Model 2		Model 3		Model 4	
	B	β	B	β	B	β	B	β
Role, interpretative (0-disseminator; 1-interpretative)							−.01	−.03
Role, adversarial (0-disseminator; 1-adversarial)							−.08***	−.13***
Role, populist-mobilizer (0-disseminator; 1-pop. mob.)							−.03	−.04
Topic, policy (0-facts; 1-policy)							−.01	−.01
Topic, reaction (0-facts; 1-reaction)							.01	.02
Topic, first-hand account (0-facts; 1-first-hand acct)							−.02	−.03
Source, expert (0-official; 1-expert)							−.03*	−.04*
Source, community (0-official; 1-community)							−.001	−.003
Source, previous victim (0-official; 1-prev. victim)							.003	.002
Source, journalist (0-official; 1-journalist)							−.07***	−.08***
Source, none (0-official; 1-no source)							−.02	−.03

Note: $R^2 = .03$ (p < .001); B – unstandardized coefficient beta; β – standardized coefficients beta; N=3,177 *p* < .05; **p* < .01; ***p<.001.
Note: negative coefficients = less neutrality.

The individual-level factor of *location* (or *physical proximity*) had a weak effect on *JF* variance even when typification and stage variables were added: broadcast journalists *closer* in physical proximity to the shooting event were more likely to have a negative *JF*, and thus have a more negative reaction nonverbally, than those *further* from the shooting event. This suggests the strongest individual-level predictor of emotional valence was location.

It's worth noting that in the full model, race, specifically for *Black* journalists, remains significant even when all other variables are considered. This suggests a stronger than expected racial factor in nonverbal neutrality. Additionally, the stages of coverage were not significant in the *JF* model, similar to the *NNS* model, offering no support for Graber's stages of crisis coverage.

The next chapter looks at how factors interacted with stages of crisis coverage.

References

Collins, S., & Long, A. (2003). Too tired to care? The psychological effects of working with trauma. *Journal of Psychiatric & Mental Health Nursing, 10*, 17–27.

Deavours, D. (2022). Nonverbal neutrality norm: How experiencing trauma affects journalists' willingness to display emotion. *Journal of Broadcast and Electronic Media, 67*(1), 112–134.

Graber, D. (2002). *Mass media and American politics* (6th ed.). CQ Press.

7 The Nonverbal Neutrality Theory

This chapter focuses on the moderating effect of stages on influences of nonverbal neutrality variability. While Graber's (2002) stages of crisis coverage theory predicts neutrality will vary in a specific pattern across the three stages of the first 24 hours of coverage, the results of H5 suggest stages are not significant direct predictors of nonverbal variability. Yet, these results suggest journalists may perform differently in each of these stages due to other influence factors, providing more nuanced understanding of routine patterns in crisis coverage. The results provide guidance on how to expand Graber's original theory to nonverbal behaviors, providing the framework for the Nonverbal Neutrality Theory.

RQ4: Individual-level factors by Graber's stages of coverage

RQ4 asks how the relationships between individual-level factors and the neutrality of nonverbal behavior vary across Graber's three stages. To test this, two-way ANOVAs were conducted. While analysis of all main effects was conducted, only the coefficients for stages of coverage are reported here, since, logically, stages as a higher-order variable (social typification) will moderate the effects of individual-level variables, rather than the other way around.

Age of shooting victims*Stages of coverage

For *NNS*, the results of the two-way ANOVA show a significant interaction between *age of victims* and *stages of coverage* for *NNS*, $F(4, 3168) = 5.03$, $p < .001$, partial $\eta2 = .01$. There was a main effect for *age* groups [$F(3, 3168) = 28.94$, $p < .001$] and *stages of coverage* [$F(2, 3168) = 20.08$, $p < .001$]. A significant difference in *NNS* by *age of victim* was found for the *second* [$F(2, 3168) = 9.21$, $p < .001$] and *third stage* [$F(2, 3168) = 26.57$, $p < .001$, partial $\eta2 = .02$], but not the *first* [$F(2, 3168) = 2.95$, $p = .05$].

Interpreting these findings, the difference in neutrality by *age of victim* is the most dramatic in the *third stage* of coverage, with the mean *NNS* much

DOI: 10.4324/9781003375340-7

higher (less neutral) for coverage of shootings with mid-range victims (M = 4.10, SD = .09) than for shootings with *younger* victims (M = 3.11, SD = .08) or *older* victims (M = 3.23, SD = .09). A similar and statistically significant pattern is found in the *second stage* of coverage.

The results suggest that the influence of the age of victim on the level of nonverbal neutrality depends on the stage of coverage, where events with younger victims are most neutral in the first stage and least neutral in the third. See Figure 7.1 for the line graph of this two-way ANOVA.

For *JF*, results of the two-way ANOVA show a significant interaction between *age of victims* and *stages of coverage* for *JF*, $F(4, 3168)$ = 3.13, p = .01. There was also a main effect for victim *age* groups [$F(2, 3168)$ = 5.78, p = .003] but not *stage of coverage* [$F(2, 3168)$ = .17, p = .85]. A significant difference in *JF* by *age of victim* was found for the *third stage* [$F(2, 3168)$ = 8.80, p < .001] but not the *first* [$F(2, 3168)$ = 1.17, p = .31] or *second* stage [$F(2, 3168)$ = 2.78, p = .06]. In the *third stage* of coverage, the difference in neutrality by *age of victim* is the most negatively valenced for coverage of shootings with the *youngest* victims (M = –.09, SD = .01) compared to shootings with both *oldest* (M = –.03, SD = .01) and *mid-range* aged victims (M = –.07, SD = .01).

Interpreting these findings, it is in the third stage of coverage that broadcasters' nonverbal behavior is most dramatically negative when covering younger victims, and these unfavorable reactions are strongest for events with young victims. Findings overall are consistent with BET predictions that shootings with younger victims will lead journalists to react more negatively, with the most negative reactions occurring in the third stage. See results in Figure 7.2.

*Number of deaths*Stages of coverage*

For *NNS*, results of the two-way ANOVA show a significant interaction between *number of deaths* and *stages of coverage* for *NNS*, $F(4, 3168)$ = 89.56, p < .001, partial $\eta2$=.01. Main effects were found for number of *deaths* [$F(2, 3168)$ = 7.03, p = .001] and *stages of coverage* [$F(2, 3168)$ = 16.83, p < .001]. A significant difference in *NNS* by *number of victims* was found for the *second* [$F(2, 3168)$ = 17.12, p < .001] and *third stage* [$F(2, 3168)$ = 4.82, p = .01], but not the *first* [$F(2, 3168)$ = 2.65, p = .07].

In the *second stage*, events with the *lowest* number of victims were least neutral (highest *NNS*) (M = 3.65, SD = .09), compared to shootings with *the highest* number of victims (M = 2.96, SD = .08) or *mid-range* number of victims (M = 3.23, SD = .09). This goes against BET-based predictions of events with more severe death tolls having less neutral coverage since those events with the lowest numbers of deaths are the least neutral.

For the *third stage*, however, the events that were least neutral (highest *NNS*) were those with the *mid-range* number of victims (M = 3.72, SD = .08),

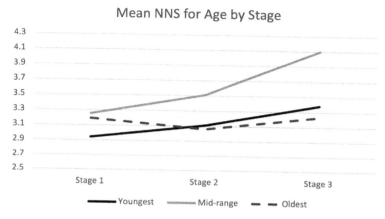

Figure 7.1 NNS means of age of victims by stage.

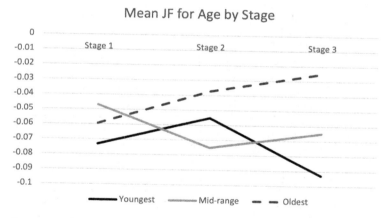

Figure 7.2 JF means of age of victims by stage.

compared to those with the *highest* ($M = 3.57$, $SD = .09$) and *lowest* ($M = 3.33$, $SD = .09$) number of victims. This shows that the severity of the event by the number of deaths has the greatest effect in the third stage of coverage. See Figure 7.3.

For *JF*, results of the two-way ANOVA show there was a significant interaction between *number of deaths* and *stages of coverage* for JF, $F(4, 3168) = 5.387$, $p < .001$, partial $\eta2 = .01$. No main effects were found for number of *deaths* [$F(2,$

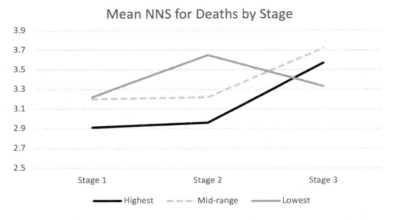

Figure 7.3 NNS means of deaths by stage.

3168) = 1.57, p = .21] or *stage of coverage* [$F(2, 3168)$] = .09, p = .91]. There was a significant difference in *JF* for coverage of shootings with different death rates for the *first* stage [$F(2, 3168)$ = 5.64, p = .004] and *third* stage [$F(2, 3168)$ = 3.09, p = .046], but not the *second* stage [$F(2, 3168)$ = 2.40, p = .09].

For the *first* stage, events with the lowest number of deaths had the lowest *JF*, or most negative nonverbal valence (M = –.08, SD = .01), compared to those with the *highest* (M = –.07, SD = .02) and *mid-range* (M = –.03, SD = .01) number of deaths. This is not consistent with BET- based predictions that events with more deaths will lead to more negative nonverbal behavior.

For the *third* stage, however, events with the *highest* number of deaths had the most negative *JF* or highest number of negative expressions (M = –.09, SD = .01), compared to those with the *mid-range* (M = –.06, SD = .01) and *lowest* (M = –.04, SD = .01) number of deaths. This reflects the BET-based predictions about the influence of severity on emotion. See Figure 7.4.

These results suggest stages may be a good moderating factor in order to understand ways in which individuals act within the routines of crisis reporting. This will be discussed further in the next chapter.

*Location*Stages of coverage*

For *NNS*, the results of the two-way ANOVA show a significant interaction between *location* and *stages* of coverage for *NNS*, $F(6, 3165)$ = 4.40, p < .001. However, no main effects were found for either *stages of coverage* or *location*. For *stages of coverage*, there was a significant difference in *NNS* for

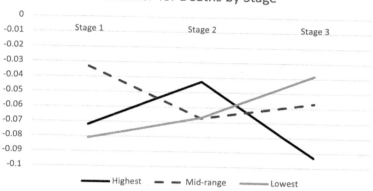

Figure 7.4 JF means of deaths by stage.

reporters' proximity for the *first* [$F(3, 3165) = 3.73$, $p = .01$, partial $\eta2 = .004$] and *second* stage [$F(3, 3165) = 4.82$, $p = .002$, partial $\eta2 = .01$], but not the *third* [$F(3, 3165) = 2.53$, $p = .06$]. For the *first* stage, *NNS* was highest (least neutral) for broadcasters reporting from a *secondary scene* ($M = 3.56$, $SD = .50$), compared to those *on scene* ($M = 3.47$, $SD = .13$), in a *newsroom* ($M = 3.08$, $SD = .06$), or at an *alternative scene* ($M = 2.75$, $SD = .24$).

Interpreting these findings, they appear consistent with BET-based predictions that nonverbal behavior will be more influenced by trauma effects, as sites close to the shooting are more likely traumatic; this is seen most dramatically in the first stage of coverage.

For the *second* stage, journalists reporting from an *alternative scene* were least neutral (highest *NNS*) ($M = 3.46$, $SD = .21$), compared to those reporting from the *newsroom* ($M = 3.38$, $SD = .07$), *secondary scene* ($M = 3.32$, $SD = .17$), and *on scene* ($M = 3.00$, $SD = .08$). This suggests that by the second stage, broadcasters who are closer to the scene become more neutral than those reporting further away from the trauma. This is consistent with BET research that suggests those who violate cultural display rules may perform masking techniques later to hide their emotions. See Figure 7.5.

For *JF*, the results of the two-way ANOVA show there was not a significant interaction between *location* and *stages* of coverage for *JF*, $F(6, 3165) = 1.67$, $p = .13$. There were no main effects for *location* [$F(3, 3165) = 2.60$, $p = .05$] or *stages of coverage* [$F(2, 3165) = .97$, $p = .38$] either. Therefore, results suggest nonverbal behavior as measured by *JF* does not differ significantly by location between stages of coverage.

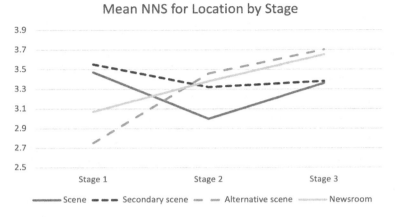

Figure 7.5 NNS means of location by stage.

*Affiliation*Stages of coverage*

For *NNS*, the results of the two-way ANOVA show there was a significant interaction between *affiliation* and *stages of coverage* for *NNS*, $F(2, 3171) =$ 6.44, $p = .002$. There was not a statistically significant main effect found for either *affiliation* or *stages of coverage*. There was a significant difference in *NNS* for stages of coverage for the *first* [$F(1, 3171) = 7.48$, $p = .01$] and *third* stages [$F(1, 3171) = 5.27$, $p = .02$], but not the *second* [$F(1, 3171) = .151$, $p = .70$].

Interpreting these findings, for the *first* stage, *local* broadcasters were the least neutral (highest *NNS*) ($M = 3.50$, $SD = .14$), compared to *national* broadcasters ($M = 3.08$, $SD = .06$). This is consistent with BET predictions that those more emotionally connected to a community will be less neutral in their nonverbal behaviors; this is seen most strongly in the first stage.

The opposite pattern was seen in the third stage, where *national* broadcasters ($M = 3.60$, $SD = .06$) were less neutral than *local* broadcasters ($M = 3.28$, $SD = .13$). This is consistent with BET-based predictions that as time goes on in the news coverage, journalists more emotionally close to the community affected will work to mask their true emotions in their nonverbal behavior. See Figure 7.6.

For *JF*, results of the two-way ANOVA show there was a statistically significant interaction between *affiliation* and *stages* of coverage for *JF*, $F(2, 3171) = 17.18$, $p < .001$. There was a main effect for *stages of coverage* [$F(2, 3171) = 7.07$, $p = .001$] but not *affiliation* [$F(1, 3171) = .28$, $p = .60$]. There was a significant difference in *JF* for stages of coverage for the *first* [$F(1,$

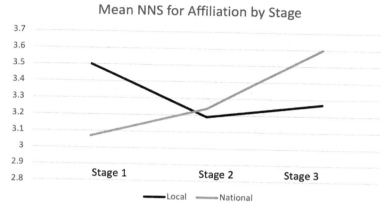

Figure 7.6 NNS means of affiliation by stage.

3171) = 19.29, $p < .001$] and *third* stages [$F(1, 3171) = 15.08, p < .001$], but not the *second* [$F(1, 3171) = .01, p = .94$]. For the *first* stage, mean *JF* was most negative and thus the least neutral for *local* broadcasters ($M = -.13, SD = .02$), compared to *national* broadcasters ($M = -.05, SD = .01$).

Interpreting these results, this is not consistent with BET predictions that those more tied to the community, and presumably more emotionally connected to the community, will experience the effects of trauma more in their nonverbal communication. The opposite pattern was found in the *third* stage, though, where the mean *JF* was most negative and thus the least neutral for *national* broadcasters ($M = -.08, SD = .01$), compared to *local* broadcasters (M = .002, $SD = .02$). This is consistent with BET theory, which suggests those closer to the event emotionally would begin nonverbal masking as coverage continues. This suggests local journalists react more negatively in stage one, while they are the most neutral in stage three; alternatively, national journalists react more negatively in stage three, while they are the most neutral in stage one. See Figure 7.7 for this.

To sum up the findings of RQ3, it appears that, for more traumatic events (those with younger victims and higher death tolls), journalists display more nonverbal neutrality during the more chaotic early coverage stage, but they tend to display the least neutrality during the third coverage stage. However, factors of proximity (being closer to the scene or more emotionally connected to the community) lead to less neutrality in the first, more chaotic stage. Also, the second stage is generally not the least neutral stage, counter to Graber's (2002) predictions.

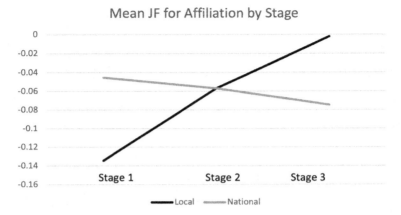

Figure 7.7 JF means of affiliation by stage.

RQ4: Social-level variables by stages

RQ4 asks how the relationships between social-level factors and the neutrality of nonverbal behavior vary across Graber's (2002) three stages. To test this, two-way ANOVAs were conducted. Analysis of all main effects is reported here to see which variables are higher-order and therefore moderating the lower-order variable.

*Role*Stages of coverage*

Descriptive statistics suggest nonneutral roles (adversarial and populist-mobilizer) occur most often in later stages, while more neutral roles (interpretative and disseminator) are more likely to occur earlier.

For *NNS*, the two-way ANOVA shows a significant interaction between role and stages of coverage for *NNS*, $F(6, 3165) = 3.15$, $p < .001$, partial $\eta2 = .01$. There was a main effect for role [$F(3, 3176) = 166.88$, $p < .001$] but not for stages of coverage [$F(2, 3177) = 2.20$, $p = .11$]. A significant difference in *NNS* by role was found for the first [$F(3, 924) = 43.74$, $p < .001$, partial $\eta2 = .13$], second [$F(3, 1180) = 62.01$, $p < .001$), partial $\eta2 = .14$], and third stages [$F(3, 1070) = 73.11$, $p < .001$), partial $\eta2 = .17$]. The difference is most significant in the third stage, with mean *NNS* higher (less neutral) for adversarial roles ($M = 4.65$, $SD = 1.42$) than populist-mobilizer ($M = 3.61$, $SD = 1.58$), interpretative ($M = 3.52$, $SD = 1.59$), and disseminator roles ($M = 2.58$, $SD = 1.59$). Similar and statistically significant patterns are found in the second and first stages. See Figure 7.8.

The results suggest that, the more nonneutral roles performed within a stage (such as adversarial), the less neutral overall the stage will be. Stage

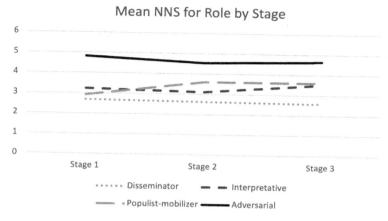

Figure 7.8 NNS means of role by stage.

three has the most nonneutral roles, followed by stage two, followed by stage one, which may at least partially explain why the neutrality of stages lessens over time. This suggests roles and stages affect nonverbal neutrality of crisis coverage, where journalists in later stages are more likely to perform nonneutral roles and thus perform more nonneutral nonverbal behaviors.

For *JF*, the two-way ANOVA suggests there is not a significant interaction between role and stages of coverage, $F(6, 3165) = 1.82$, $p = .09$. While there is a main effect for role [$F(3, 3176) = 24.28$, $p < .001$], there is not a significant main effect for stages [$F(2, 3177) = 1.26$, $p = .28$]. A significant difference in *JF* by role was found for the first [$F(3, 924) = 11.85$, $p < .001$, partial $\eta2 = .04$], second [$F(3, 1180) = 8.65$, $p < .001$, partial $\eta2 = .02$], and third stages [$F(3, 1070) = 6.26$, $p < .001$, partial $\eta2 = .02$]. The difference in neutrality by role is the most dramatic in the first stage of coverage, with the mean *JF* much lower (less neutral) for adversarial roles ($M = -.18$, $SD = .18$) than for populist-mobilizer ($M = -.07$, $SD = .21$), interpretative ($M = -.04$, $SD = .23$), and disseminator roles ($M = -.04$, $SD = .17$). Similar and statistically significant patterns are found in the second and third stages of coverage as well. See Figure 7.9.

The results suggest that the more nonneutral roles performed within a stage (such as adversarial), the more negative and less neutral overall the stage will be. However, there are fewer differentiations in the more neutral roles (interpretative and disseminator) for *JF*, lessening its effect. This suggests there may be patterns of roles and stages affecting nonverbal neutrality of crisis coverage, particularly as broadcasters in later stages are more likely to perform nonneutral roles and thus react more negatively in their nonverbal

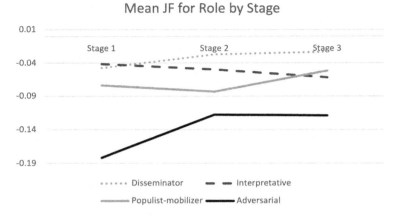

Figure 7.9 JF means of role by stage.

behaviors. This may also suggest that the adversarial role may lend itself to negative nonverbal behavior.

*Framing*Stages of coverage*

Descriptive statistics suggest episodic and episodic-thematic framing occurred most frequently across the three stages. Yet, thematic and thematic-episodic framing occurred more in later stages than earlier ones.

For *NNS*, the two-way ANOVA suggests framing by stage does not have a statistically significant effect on the nonverbal neutrality score. There is no significant interaction between framing and stages of coverage for *NNS*, $F(6, 3165) = .44$, $p = .85$. However, there was a main effect for frame [$F(3, 3176) = 93.96$, $p < .001$] and for stages of coverage [$F(2, 3177) = 4.75$, $p = .01$]. A significant difference in *NNS* by frame was found for the first [$F(3, 924) = 24.32$, $p < .001$, partial $\eta2 = .07$], second [$F(3, 1180) = 38.97$, $p < .001$, partial $\eta2 = .09$], and third stages [$F(3, 1070) = 38.85$, $p < .001$, partial $\eta2 = .10$]. The difference in neutrality by frame is the most dramatic in the third stage of coverage, with the mean *NNS* much higher (less neutral) for thematic framing ($M = 5.13$, $SD = 1.22$) than for thematic-episodic ($M = 4.29$, $SD = 1.42$), episodic-thematic ($M = 4.09$, $SD = 1.55$), and episodic framing ($M = 3.22$, $SD = 1.68$). Similar and statistically significant patterns are found in the second and first stages of coverage as well. See Figure 7.10.

The results suggest that, the more thematic framing that occurs within a stage, the less neutral overall the stage will be. This suggests journalists in later stages are more likely to utilize thematic framing, which may make their coverage less neutral overall.

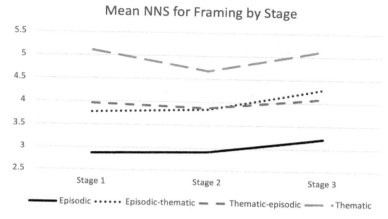

Figure 7.10 NNS means of framing by stage.

For *JF*, the two-way ANOVA suggests frame by stage does have a statistically significant effect. There is a significant interaction between frame and stages of coverage for *JF*, $F(6, 3165) = 3.61$, p = .001, partial $\eta2 = .01$. There was a significant main effect for frame for *JF* [$F(3, 3176) = 17.10$, p < .001] and for stages of coverage [$F(2, 3177) = 6.94$, $p < .001$]. A significant difference in *JF* by role was found for the first [$F(3, 924) = 9.49, p < .001$, partial $\eta2 = .0$] and third stages [$F(3, 1070) = 11.39, p < .001$, partial $\eta2 = .03$], but not the second stage [$F(3, 1180) = 2.27, p = .08$]). The most significant difference was in the third stage where the most negative and thus least neutral frame was thematic ($M = -.28, SD = .48$), thematic-episodic ($M = -.07, SD = .27$), episodic-thematic ($M = -.07, SD = .24$), and episodic ($M = -.05, SD = .22$). Similar and significant patterns were found in stage one, but stage two showed less difference in *JF* across the four framing types, which is why it was not significant. See Figure 7.11.

This suggests there may be patterns of framing and stages affecting the nonverbal neutrality of crisis coverage, where journalists in later stages are more likely to utilize thematic framing that may make their overall presentation more negative emotionally.

Topic*Stages of coverage

Descriptive statistics suggest topics varied across the stages. Facts were most common earlier in coverage, specifically the second and first stages; policy was most often used in later stages, specifically the third and second stages. First-hand accounts and reactions were most common in the second stage

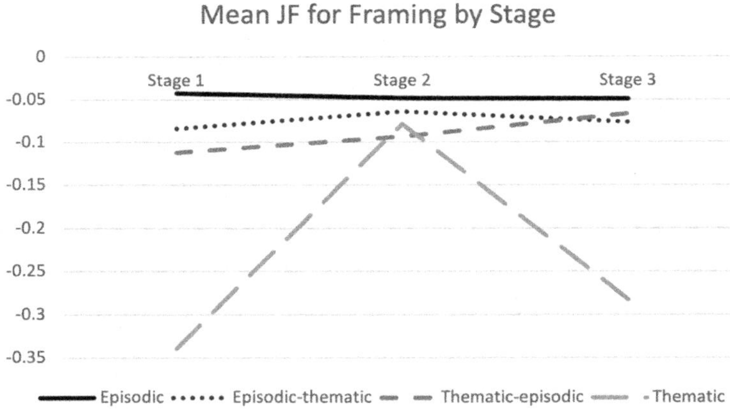

Mean JF for Framing by Stage

Figure 7.11 JF means of framing by stage.

followed by the third. This suggests an early reliance on facts-based topics in the first stage and then more policy-based discussions in later stages.

For *NNS*, the results of the two-way ANOVA show a significant interaction, $F(11, 3165) = 26.95$, $p < .001$. There were main effects for topic [$F(3, 3165) = 77.56$, $p < .001$] and stages of coverage [$F(2, 3165) = 13.18$, $p < .001$]. For stages of coverage, there was a significant difference in *NNS* for topic for the first stage [$F(3, 925) = 19.86$, $p < .001$, partial $\eta2 = .06$], second stage [$F(3, 1181) = 34.05$, $p < .001$, partial $\eta2 = .08$], and third stage [$F(3, 1071) = 32.79$, $p < .001$, partial $\eta2 = .09$]. For the first stage, *NNS* was lowest (most neutral) for topics of facts (n = 519, $M = 2.90$, $SD = 1.67$), then first-hand accounts (n = 147, $M = 2.95$, $SD = 1.73$), then reactions (n = 103, $M = 3.20$, $SD = 1.61$), and policy was the highest (least neutral) (n = 156, $M = 4.06$, $SD = 1.69$). For the second stage, *NNS* was lowest (most neutral) for topics of fact (n = 540, $M = 2.87$, $SD = 1.59$), then reactions (n = 134, $M = 2.95$, $SD = 1.53$), then first-hand accounts (n = 234, $M = 3.37$, $SD = 1.38$), and policy was the highest (least neutral) (n = 264, $M = 4.00$, $SD = 1.54$). For the third stage, *NNS* was lowest (most neutral) for topics of facts (n = 441, $M = 3.11$, $SD = 1.73$), then first-hand accounts (n = 207, $M = 3.28$, $SD = 1.51$), then reactions (n = 116, $M = 3.95$, $SD = 1.66$), and policy was the highest or least neutral topic (n = 307, $M = 4.23$, $SD = 1.53$). See Figure 7.12.

These findings show facts are always the most neutral topic for *NNS*, while policy is always the least neutral topic. It is interesting to note that as the event progresses, journalists are more likely to discuss policy, the least neutral topic.

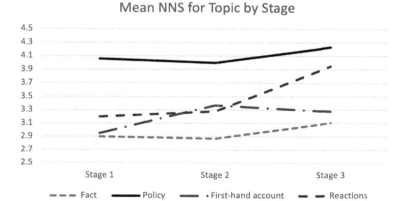

Figure 7.12 Mean NNS of topic by stage.

For *JF* the results of the two-way ANOVA show a significant interaction, $F(11, 3165) = 4.20$, $p < .001$. There were main effects for topic [$F(3, 3165)$ = 11.39, $p < .001$] but not stages of coverage [$F(2, 3165) = .48$, $p = .62$]. For stages of coverage, there was a significant difference in *JF* for topic for the first stage [$F(3, 925) = 5.60$, $p < .001$, partial $\eta2 = .02$], second stage [$F(3, 1181) = 3.40$, $p = .02$, partial $\eta2 = .01$], and third stage [$F(3, 1071) = 5.69$, $p < .001$, partial $\eta2 = .02$]. For the first stage, *JF* was highest (most neutral) for topics of reaction ($M = -.04$, $SD = .18$), then first-hand accounts ($M = -.04$, SD = .29), then facts ($M = -.05$, $SD = .20$), and policy was the lowest (most negative/least neutral) ($M = -.12$, $SD = .22$). For the second stage, *JF* was highest (most neutral) for topics of fact ($M = -.04$, $SD = .16$), then first-hand accounts ($M = -.06$, $SD = .20$), then reaction ($M = -.07$, $SD = .17$), and policy was the lowest (most negative/least neutral) ($M = -.08$, $SD = .26$). For the third stage, *JF* was highest (most neutral) for topics of first-hand accounts ($M = -.03$, SD = .22), then facts ($M = -.04$, $SD = .28$), then policy ($M = -.10$, $SD = .28$), and reactions was the lowest (most negative/least neutral) topic ($M = -.10$, $SD =$ .32). See Figure 7.13.

These findings suggest that nonverbal neutrality by topic fluctuates across the event; most notably facts are the second least neutral topic in the first stage and then get more neutral as the event progresses. Alternatively, policy starts off the least neutral, gets more neutral in the second stage, and becomes less neutral in the third stage. These findings suggest journalists' emotionality nonverbally fluctuates by topic across the event and shows patterns based on topics.

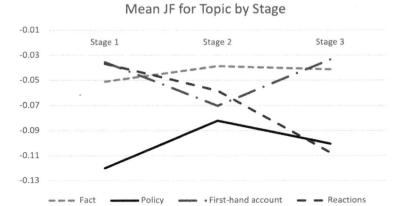

Figure 7.13 Mean JF of topic by stage.

*Sources*Stages of coverage*

Similar patterns are seen through the two-way ANOVAs for sources. Descriptives suggest that while journalists always use officials most often in all three stages, they rely heavily on officials in the first stage, but diversify their sources in the second and third stages, relying more heavily on experts and journalists in the third stage.

For *NNS*, there is a significant interaction, $F(11, 3165) = 18.63, p < .001$, partial $\eta2 = .09$. There were main effects for source [$F(5, 3165) = 48.71, p < .001$, partial $\eta2 = .07$] and stages of coverage [$F(2, 3165) = 4.38, p = .01$]. For stages of coverage, there was a significant difference in *NNS* for source for the first stage [$F(5, 925) = 9.42, p < .001$, partial $\eta2 = .05$], second stage [$F(5, 1181) = 19.44, p < .001$, partial $\eta2 = .08$], and third stage [$F(5, 1071) = 27.51, p < .001$, partial $\eta2 = .11$]. For the first stage, *NNS* was lowest (most neutral) when journalists used no source (n = 208, $M = 2.72, SD = 1.69$), then officials (n = 393, $M = 3.07, SD = 1.72$), communities (n = 159, $M = 3.15, SD = 1.64$), experts (n = 90, $M = 3.46, SD = 1.62$), previous victim (n = 8, $M = 4.00, SD = 1.69$), and media were the highest (least neutral) (n = 67, $M = 4.24, SD = 1.67$). In the second stage, *NNS* was lowest (most neutral) when journalists used no source (n = 262, $M = 2.92, SD = 1.63$), then officials (n = 382, $M = 3.03, SD = 1.50$), communities (n = 280, $M = 3.08, SD = 1.47$), previous victims (n = 35, $M = 3.63, SD = 1.42$), experts (n = 125, $M = 3.93, SD = 1.60$), and journalists were the highest (least neutral) (n = 97, $M = 4.32, SD = 1.58$). In the third stage, *NNS* was lowest (most neutral) when journalists used no source (n = 203, $M = 2.64, SD = 1.69$), then officials (n = 341, M

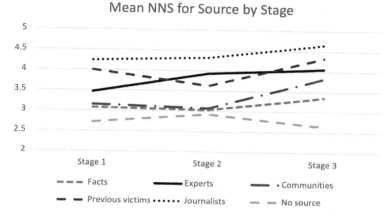

Figure 7.14 Mean NNS of source by stage.

= 3.35, SD = 1.64), communities (n = 258, M = 3.82, SD = 1.54), experts (n = 178, M = 4.06, SD = 1.64), previous victims (n = 9, M = 4.33, SD = 1.32), and journalists were the highest (least neutral) (n = 82, M = 4.65, SD = 1.29). See Figure 7.14.

These findings suggest no source, officials, and communities are always the lowest *NNS* and thus the most neutral, while journalists citing themselves, experts, or previous victims are the least neutral with the highest *NNS*.

For *JF* the results of the two-way ANOVA show a significant interaction, $F(17, 3159) = 3.51, p < .001$. There were main effects for source [$F(5, 3159) = 9.12, p < .001$] but not stages of coverage [$F(2, 3159) = 1.37, p = .26$] (Figure 7.4). For stages of coverage, there was a significant difference in *JF* for source for the first stage [$F(5, 924) = 3.15, p = .01$, partial $\eta2 = .02$], second stage [$F(5, 1175) = 5.09, p < .001$, partial $\eta2 = .02$], and third stage [$F(5, 1065) = 3.76, p = .002$, partial $\eta2 = .02$]. For the first stage, *JF* was closest to zero (most neutral) when journalists used no source ($M = -.04, SD = .18$), previous victims ($M = +.05, SD = .13$), communities ($M = -.05, SD = .27$), officials ($M = -.06, SD = .18$), experts ($M = -.07, SD = .21$), and journalists were the lowest (most negative/least neutral) ($M = -.15, SD = .28$). In the second stage, *JF* was closest to zero (most neutral) when journalists used officials ($M = -.03, SD = .16$), no source ($M = -.05, SD = .17$), communities ($M = -.05, SD = .20$), experts ($M = -.08, SD = .26$), previous victims ($M = -.11, SD = .26$), and journalists were the lowest (most negative/least neutral) ($M = -.13, SD = .27$). In the third stage, *JF* was closest to zero (most neutral) when journalists used officials ($M = -.04, SD = .20$), no source ($M = -.04, SD = .20$), previous victims ($M = +.04, SD = .31$), communities ($M = -.06, SD = .29$), experts

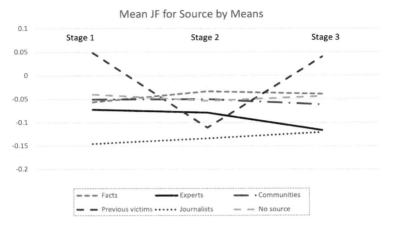

Figure 7.15 Mean JF of source by stage.

($M = -.12$, $SD = .31$), and journalists were the lowest (most negative/least neutral) ($M = -.12$, $SD = .27$). See Figure 7.15.

These findings suggest most sources have similar *JF* means regardless of stage. The largest fluctuation is previous victims where journalists in the first and third stages show positive nonverbal behaviors while in the second stage they display negative nonverbal behavior. Overall, though, journalists sourcing officials, communities, or no sources are more neutral, while those using experts, previous victims, and journalists are nonneutral and have negative displays.

To sum up the findings of RQ4, it appears later stages support typifications that are less nonverbally neutral, where journalists display more nonverbal neutrality during more chaotic early coverage stages. These results also give more insight into how these routine typifications of journalistic work play out over the first 24 hours of a crisis. This can help journalists, media organizations, and educators discern whether these coverage patterns are beneficial and help training with best practices.

Nonverbal Neutrality Theory

The findings of this study provide the basis for a new theory, termed the Nonverbal Neutrality Theory here. The theory seeks to explain the predictive powers of individual- and social-level factors on nonverbal neutrality, both in terms of expressiveness and valence.

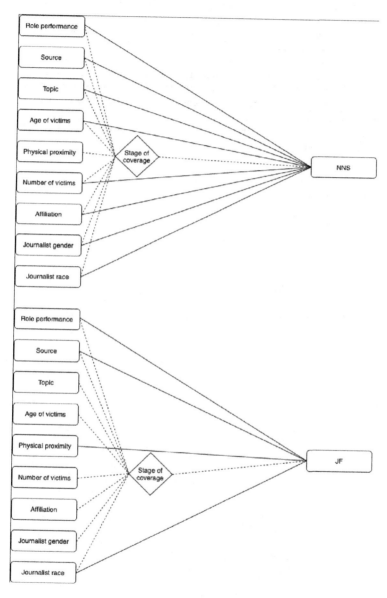

Figure 7.16 Nonverbal Neutrality Theory.

Framing was left out of the total theory flowchart as it did not have enough significance for *NNS* or *JF* in the models to be considered. Additionally, stages were not tested as a moderating factor for gender or race, since a reporter's demographics would not change across stages.

A flow chart of the theory is presented in Figure 7.16.

This theory flow chart allows scholars to understand the ways in which each factor predicts *NNS* and/or *JF*, and whether the predictions become stronger when moderated through stages. This theory provides insight into the ways in which journalists' nonverbal neutrality will vary during crisis coverage.

The applications for this theory and the other findings are addressed further in the next chapter.

Reference

Graber, D. (2002). *Mass media and American politics* (6th ed.). CQ Press.

8 Understanding nonverbal neutrality variability

This work advances Graber's (2002) stages of crisis coverage theory through the application of two nonverbal theories, Basic Emotions Theory (BET) and Behavioral Ecology of Facial Expressions (BECV), as they relate to broadcasters' nonverbal communication during crisis. It examines the factors that influence variability in journalists' nonverbal neutrality and emotionality. Graber's theory shows how journalists work when facing emotional trauma, predicting patterns of behavior. This study builds on that framework to show the various factors, at both the individual and social level, that affect the nonverbal reactions of journalists in these situations, and thus overall neutrality. The expanded Nonverbal Neutrality Theory allows scholars to better understand what shapes the nonverbal behaviors of journalists in these situations, filling a gap in the current theoretical framework.

A broad view of the findings suggests that, overall, broadcast journalists are less likely to adhere to the professional norm of neutrality in their nonverbal behavior during crises. In looking at means for the two dimensions of nonverbal neutrality, *NNS* and *JF*, broadcasters show more nonneutral movements than neutral ones and display more negatively valenced reactions in those behaviors than neutral or positive emotions. This suggests deviance from the norm of nonverbal neutrality (Deavours, 2022), and this work has sought explanations for those deviations through the exploration of individual- and social-level factors of influence.

Typifications' influence on nonverbal neutrality

The factors that cause the most variance in both dimensions of nonverbal neutrality are typifications. Since journalism is a profession that relies on standards of practice and normative behavior as a distinguishing factor (Schudson, 2001), these typifications impact all aspects of the newsgathering process. This study shows that those standards of practice and their impact on objectivity extend to nonverbal behavior. Typifications allow broadcasters to have increased certainty in uncertain situations, so it is understandable that as journalists face trauma and crisis, they may rely more heavily on what they

DOI: 10.4324/9781003375340-8

know – socially constructed professional norms. Depending on the adherence of that typification to objectivity standards, nonverbal neutrality varies.

According to the regressions, role performance is one of the strongest predictors of nonverbal neutrality, both in terms of neutrality of movement and valence of behavior. Role performance is linked to role conceptualization, and the way a journalist thinks about his or her work can greatly influence the desire to adhere to certain professional standards, especially objectivity (Weaver et al., 2019). H8 finds *NNS* and *JF* vary significantly based on what role a journalist is performing, where disseminator roles are the most neutral and adversarial roles are the least neutral. Broadcasters performing roles that emphasize objectivity as a central function of work, like disseminators, are more likely to work to remain neutral nonverbally even in crisis. Those performing roles that allow for greater subjectivity, like adversarial roles, are less likely to remain nonverbally neutral. This suggests that even though most standards of objectivity and neutrality do not explicitly discuss nonverbal behavior (Deavours, 2022), journalists still vary nonverbal communication based on these professional norms. These findings also support a BECV approach, which predicts journalists are not merely reacting to stimuli; they are also working, consciously or unconsciously, to shape their nonverbal behaviors to conform to social and professional expectations.

The influence of typification factors is further emphasized through another strong predictor of neutrality: source. While one may intuitively expect journalists to be more emotional when speaking to victims and those affected by crisis, RQ2 finds journalists show no statistical difference in emotional valence whether they are talking to victims or officials. Instead, it is when journalists are talking to experts of policy reform or speaking from their personal experiences that they show significantly less neutrality. This likely happens because journalists are often trained to interview and speak to victims neutrally in everyday situations like car crashes and smaller-scale crimes, beginning early in journalism school; so when journalists need to speak to victims during crises, they rely on standard typifications of practice that are more neutral. Yet, having journalism students or early career professionals involved in discussions of policy or providing their first-person witness accounts is less routinized in journalism (Aitamurto & Varma, 2019). When journalists serve as their own sources and cite their own experience, or use expert sources to interpret policy, they put themselves in contexts for which they have less training or preparation in terms of practicing neutrality norms; because they do not have that typified, routinized experience from which to draw, they may be more likely to display less neutral nonverbal behavior.

Topics are the final typification that showed influence on both *NNS* and *JF* (see RQ1). Broadcasters who discussed facts were most likely to be nonverbally neutral, while journalists who were discussing topics of policy were the most likely to be nonneutral and negatively valenced in their nonverbal expressions. Since the objectivity norm outlines reliance on facts as a key element of its definition, this has external validity. Policy topics were a significant predictor of *NNS* and *JF* in both regression models (see Tables 6.11 and 6.12).

A key function of objectivity is to help journalists avoid swaying political debate (Vos, 2011), which is why policy topics being the least neutral is interesting. Journalists report having no tolerance for nonverbal nonneutrality in political coverage (Deavours, 2022). Yet, studies suggest nonneutral nonverbal presentations are prevalent in everyday political journalism (Banning & Coleman, 2009), so these findings may have implications beyond just crisis journalism. It also suggests broadcasters may have less of a framework to rely upon in crisis when discussing political or cultural issues and their solutions, which may lead to less neutral nonverbal communication.

Findings were mixed for framing, a typification factor that significantly influenced *NNS* and *JF* (see H9) but was not significant in the regression when controlling for all factors. Journalists who framed their coverage to focus on the event itself in an episodic way were more likely to display neutral nonverbal behavior, while journalists who covered more thematic issues, such as those involving policy or proliferation of school shootings, were more likely to display nonneutral behavior, both in terms of expression and valence. Framing experts (Iyengar, 1991) suggest episodic topics will be covered more insularly, and this allows journalists to focus on the facts of the case, leading to more objective coverage; alternatively, thematic coverage encourages journalists to step away from the event and move toward related policies, social issues, and connections between events, which may be more subjective and speculative. It wasn't included in the final theory due to its lack of overall significance, but it is still something to be discussed due to its impact on some nonverbal neutrality aspects.

These findings support a link between the typified practices of objectivity and nonverbal neutrality, something previously studied primarily in linguistic forms. This suggests broadcasters need to be more aware of their nonverbal behaviors and their potential to impact bias perceptions. In addition, these typification findings establish evidence that broadcasters who follow professional norms in crisis are more likely to be neutral. Berkowitz (1992) says that, during "what-a-story" coverage, where uncertainty may be higher due to the unusual context of the story, broadcasters will rely on typifications to control their work and be more efficient. As similar types of crisis events, like school shootings, occur, these patterns of how to do work become solidified and so routine that journalists often unconsciously replicate those practices. In my interviews with broadcasters (2022), I found journalists often focus on "getting the job done" as a coping mechanism for the emotional chaos of a crisis, and what they may actually be referring to is focusing on routine patterns to work more efficiently. Future studies should explore other routine practices of journalism, such as breaking news or live coverage, to see if these patterns hold. This is further support for BECV, which suggests social expectations, rather than emotional reaction to stimuli, influence nonverbal communication most.

Individual factors of influence

However, journalists are not robots, bound to routine professional norms alone; they have individual autonomy to make decisions and react. That means journalists are also being influenced by individual-level factors, although findings suggest to a lesser degree than social factors. Some individual-level factors were significant in the regression, though, suggesting some BET-predicted nonverbal reactions to traumatic stimuli.

NNS and *JF* varied significantly by the age of victims. Results from H1 support BET-level conclusions for the valence of emotional expression (*JF*), where broadcasters reporting from events with younger victims are more likely to display negative emotional valences. This supports a BET perspective, suggesting the event severity affects the valence of journalists' displays.

The same pattern is not seen for *NNS* in the ANOVA findings, where events with mid-range victims are the most nonneutral. However, when the three categories of age (youngest, mid-range, and oldest) were recoded as a dichotomous variable in the *NNS* regression model, the findings flip, and events with younger victims have higher *NNS* and thus less neutral coverage than events with older victims. This is consistent with BET. Since broadcasters likely do not think of age in three distinct categories, but rather the more simplified older and younger victims, this may be the better, more valid measure. This also suggests future researchers need to consider how they are measuring the age of victims.

The age of victims was not significant in the final regression model for *JF*, pointing to a stronger influence of other factors once typifications, demographics, and stages are considered. This suggests an interplay between these individual and social variables.

The number of victims is also a measure of severity in crisis, but findings do not support predictions from trauma theory or BET. *JF* is not significantly affected by the number of victims, while *NNS* does vary significantly, but not in the predicted direction. While more deaths should mean less neutral behavior according to BET and trauma research (Xu & Li, 2012), events with the lowest number of deaths have the highest *NNS* and thus the least neutral coverage; this is seen in the *NNS* regression model as well, where the number of victims remains significant, but not in the expected direction (see Table 6.11). There are a number of potential explanations for the lack of variability for *JF* and for a higher death rate correlating with more neutrality for *NNS*. These include journalists relying more heavily on objective typification routines during severe events (Phipps & Byrne, 2003) and the ability for journalists to compartmentalize and be desensitized to death (Deavours, 2022). Also, journalists may not know the true death toll until later in coverage as details about the event continue to come out.

Another individual-level factor was proximity, conceptualized in terms of physical, emotional, and chronemic closeness to the event. Analysis for physical proximity (H3) showed no significance for either *NNS* or *JF*. However, physical proximity, or location, was a significant, although weak, predictor of *JF* in the regression model (Table 6.12), where those closer to the scene were less neutral than those further away. Because the regression model used a dichotomous variable rather than the four categories of location that the ANOVA did, this may have influenced its predictive strength. But the overall prediction of BET is seen: the closer to trauma, the more negative the expressions of the broadcaster may be. This supports a BET approach, where journalists show more negativity in their nonverbal expressions because they are reacting to the traumatic stimuli around them. Future scholars should use the dichotomous measure.

The second factor of proximity, emotional proximity – conceptualized as "affiliation" or whether the broadcaster was local or national – was not significant for *NNS* or *JF* when other factors were included (see H4). However, affiliation was a significant, although weak, predictor of *NNS* in the regression model (Table 6.11). Yet, it was national rather than local broadcasters who were the least neutral. This finding is inconsistent with BET.

The third factor of proximity, chronemic proximity or stage of coverage, was not significant in any of the ANOVAs or regressions in the predicted directions. Despite finding support for distinct stages of coverage, there is no indication of broadcasters returning to more neutral levels in later stages of coverage as Graber (2002) predicts in the stages of crisis coverage theory and that Coleman and Wu's (2006) found in their study of 9/11 coverage. This suggests the predicted theoretical pattern does not hold for every type of crisis. However, it is possible that an inverted U shape would have emerged if a wider range of hours had been sampled for these cases.

Perhaps broadcasters reporting during school shooting coverage, which is becoming increasingly routine and complex, need more time to return to professional standards of objectivity. Coleman and Wu (2006) used 9/11 as a case study to empirically test Graber's theory. 9/11 was a terrorist event with a clear outside enemy, potentially allowing for a more unified media message in the third stage. Alternatively, school shootings may not have a culprit that is as clearly agreed-upon or defined. This may suggest a need for longer adversarial and interpretative stages to debate what people, organizations, and policies are most to blame for the crisis. A political split in messaging may lead to a longer period of nonneutrality, and so extend the pattern further out, chronemically. Future studies could extend the timing of the sample to see when nonverbal neutrality returns later, as Graber and vicarious traumatization research predict.

Demographic variables of gender and race were significant. Results from H6 show female broadcasters are more nonverbally nonneutral than males for *NNS*, and this factor remains significant in the regression model when other factors are added (see Table 6.11). Yet, it is not significant for *JF*, either in H6 or the *JF* regression model, suggesting the difference is not in emotionality, but in the broadcasters' expressiveness. This supports previous research that finds women tend to be more expressive than males (Hall, 1984), and it may also suggest nonverbal neutrality is influenced more by the social norms of gender than by individual gender traits. It may also suggest that women are more strongly constrained by journalism professional norms than men. They may use them as a way to overcome their minority status in newsrooms and legitimize their place in the profession by following normative practices (Tuchman, 1978).

Similarly, race, particularly for *Black* reporters compared to white reporters, remains significant in both the *NNS* and *JF* regression models, when considering all other variables. These findings bolster previous research showing that cultural norms for racial groups affect overall expressiveness (Matsumoto, 1993). As with women, Black journalists might feel more constrained by professional norms of objectivity, feeling pressure based on discrimination to be less autonomous and to follow professional norms (Tuchman, 1978). Future studies should explore potential explanations for these nonverbal differences of broadcaster gender and race.

Routinization patterns by stages

The results of using stage as a moderating factor for the variables suggest objective typification factors (like disseminator role performance, episodic framing, facts-based topics, and official sources) are associated with more severe cases and in earlier stages. This could point to journalists using these objective practices more often when cases are more severe, a way of coping with the trauma. In the face of the initial chaos and uncertainty of a school shooting, broadcasters may rely more heavily on typifications to get the job done, compartmentalizing their feelings in order to work more efficiently. This is one of the benefits of typifications (Berkowitz, 1992): they allow crisis workers to run on autopilot so they can function despite trauma. Yet, as time goes on, they display less neutral behavior, whether because of the effects of the trauma catching up to them, or due to the increased reliance on less objective typifications like adversarial role performance, policy-driven topics, and expert-sourced coverage. Since these factors of typification also predict less neutral behavior, it is unsurprising then that the stages themselves would also be less neutral as time progresses (seen in findings for *NNS* in H5). This suggests broadcasters are able to control their nonverbal behaviors in earlier stages by adhering to traditional work routines that encourage objectivity, especially in more severe cases, but as the event progresses, they are less likely to follow these patterns. Therefore, theoretical conceptualizations of stages should take typifications of work patterns into account.

Additionally, these more severe cases may become exceptions for standard practices. They allow for less neutral presentations, and so they appear to be "gray space" in the normally black-and-white conceptions of the professional norm of neutrality. In my qualitative interviews with professional journalists (2022), I found members of the industry tend to give exceptions to journalists who show emotion while reporting on events with young victims and instances of high death rates. While these journalists expected their professional peers to quickly return to standard expectations of neutrality, respondents were more understanding when journalists showed emotions or biased behaviors in these cases, suggesting ongoing boundary negotiation with nonverbal neutrality norms. As individuals help construct social norms, these predictors at the individual level could be interacting with the social-level factors, and reliance on norms may vary in certain cases. Media sociologists should explore this interrelationship further in future research.

However, the emotional influence of trauma has an impact when looking across stages as well. Results in RQ4 for proximity factors of location and affiliation suggest vicarious traumatization may still affect nonverbal neutrality, both for facial movements and emotional valence, where broadcasters closer to more severe trauma are more likely to be expressive and negatively valenced at first. As the effects of that trauma decline, perhaps because desensitization occurs or because they revert to more objective practices, the broadcasters who were initially nonneutral and negatively valenced work to become more neutral in their nonverbal presentations.

Alternatively, those not as close to the event start more neutral, especially in contrast to the sometimes overt displays of emotion expressed by local journalists or those closer to the scene; but in later stages, those less close become less neutral, perhaps because of an increased reliance on less objective typification practices (like adversarial role performance, thematic framing, policy topics, and journalists as sources), which are seen more in later stages in the post-hoc chi-squares. This provides evidence for BET and vicarious trauma-related effects, despite the stronger influence of BECV-related factors in the total regression models.

These factors are important to consider for these events because there is the potential for professional norms to routinize and become implicitly understood expectations for future events, shifts in the negotiated boundaries of professional norms. Looking across events (see Table 6.2), earlier events like Columbine, Virginia Tech, and Sandy Hook have lower nonverbal neutrality scores, suggesting more neutral presentations, while those that occurred later like Umpqua, Santa Fe, and Parkland have higher scores and thus less neutral presentations. This potentially shows that as these events continue and become more routine, journalists may adhere to nonverbal neutrality standards less and less, although there are too few cases to know if this is part of a larger pattern. If this were representative of a larger pattern, it could be because of the increased need for thematic connections as more shootings happen, frustrations of the events continuing without policy change, and/or the emotional toll of reporting on continued traumatic events.

Additionally, as professional boundaries of neutrality in a previous event shift to allow for less neutral behavior to be seen as more acceptable, journalists may not work as hard to control their nonverbal movements to meet those original standards of objectivity, relying on the most recent normative boundaries. This supports a BECV approach, which would suggest that as standards of acceptable neutrality change in the field, so too will the nonverbal behaviors to meet those goals in future events.

Nonverbal Neutrality Theory

This study also provides a multi-level analysis, finding interplay between individual and social levels as well. This is especially evident in the findings of RQ4 and RQ5, which looks at how *NNS* and *JF* vary by individual factors by stage. Factors that were not significant in the one-way ANOVAs (like number of deaths for *JF*; location for *NNS*; and affiliation for *NNS* and *JF*) were significant when considering stages of coverage.

This led to expanding Graber's (2002) original stages of crisis coverage theory, which was first extended by Coleman and Wu (2006) to include nonverbal neutrality, by exploring various factors of influence rather than just stages. This helps the theory's robustness and ability to generalize to other content. Additionally, it considers factors across various stages of influence and is based on nonverbal theory, allowing for a more nuanced understanding of how nonverbal neutrality varies in crisis coverage.

Scholars can utilize this theory to predict influences on nonverbal neutrality by individual- and social-level influences. This theory also predicts ways in which stages may influence variability in broadcaster nonverbal variability, utilizing it as a moderating factor for stronger influences.

This theory can be utilized in other crisis contexts, such as manmade disasters, war coverage, and political protest coverage, as well as in traditional coverage patterns. While some factors may need to be modified outside of crisis contexts, such as event severity, future scholars could explore other influences in these contexts to make the theory even more robust. Additionally, the theory needs to be tested in journalism systems, such as those that do not rely on objectivity as the normative standard, and internationally where cultural display rules may affect nonverbal neutrality.

Conclusion

Overall, these results show that broadcasters display more nonneutral nonverbal behaviors and negative expressions compared to neutral ones overall.

Typifications are the strongest predictor of that variability, regardless of whether measuring muscle movements or emotional valence. Yet, there is still evidence of the effects of vicarious traumatization present, suggesting an interplay between individual and social levels. This suggests academics and media professionals need to consider the impacts of factors at all levels of analysis in order to better understand nonverbal neutrality during crises.

The results of this study help confirm previous findings (i.e. Coleman & Wu, 2006; Zimmerman, 2014) that nonverbal displays of broadcasters vary significantly, despite journalists' efforts to maintain certain standards of neutrality. By adding these factors of analysis across various levels, the findings provide a starting place for other researchers to continue to explore influences on the nonverbal communication of broadcasters. Providing a more comprehensive approach to understanding journalistic neutrality through the application of nonverbal theories, this theory contributes to a better understanding of the patterns of how journalists nonverbally communicate during crises.

Applications to research, the field, and journalism education are discussed in the next chapter.

References

Aitamurto, T., & Varma, A. (2019). The constructive role of journalism: Contentious metadiscourse on constructive journalism and solutions journalism. *Journalism Practice*, *12*(6), 695–713.

Banning, S., & Coleman, R. (2009). Louder than words: A content analysis of presidential candidates' televised nonverbal communication. *Visual Communication Quarterly*, *16*(1), 4–17.

Berkowitz, D. (1992). Routine newswork and the what-a-story: A case study of organizational adaptation. *Journal of Broadcasting & Electronic Media*, *36*(1), 45–61.

Coleman, R., & Wu, D. (2006, June 7). More than words alone: Incorporating broadcasters' nonverbal communication into the stages of crisis coverage theory –evidence from September 11. *Journal of Broadcasting & Electronic Media*, *50*(1), 1–17.

Deavours, D. (2022). Nonverbal neutrality norm: How experiencing trauma affects journalists' willingness to display emotion. *Journal of Broadcast and Electronic Media*, *67*(1), 112–134.

Graber, D. (2002). *Mass media and American politics* (6th ed.). CQ Press.

Hall, J. (1984). *Nonverbal sex differences: Communication accuracy and expressive style*. John Hopkins University Press.

Iyengar, S. (1991). The media game: New moves, old strategies. *Press, Politics, and Political Science*, *9*(1), 1–6.

Matsumoto, D. (1993). Ethnic differences in affect intensity, emotion judgments, display rule attitudes, and self-reported emotional expression in an American sample. *Motivation and Emotion*, *17*(2), 107–123.

Phipps, A., & Byrne, M. (2003). Brief interventions for secondary trauma: Review and recommendations. *Stress and Health*, *19*, 139–147.

Schudson, M. (2001). The objectivity norm in American journalism. *Journalism*, *2*(2), 149–170.

Tuchman, G. (1978). Professionalism as an agent of legitimation. *Journal of Communication, 28*(2), 106–113.

Weaver, D.H., Willnat, L., & Wilhoit, G.C. (2019). The American journalist in the digital age: Another look at U.S. news people. *Journalism & Mass Communication Quarterly, 96*(1), 101–130.

Vos, T. P. (2011). "A mirror of the times": A history of the mirror metaphor in journalism. *Journalism Studies, 12*(5), 575–589.

Xu, K., & Li, W. (2012). An ethical stakeholder approach to crisis communication: A case study of Foxconn's 2010 employee suicide crisis. *Journal of Business Ethics, 117*(2), 371–386.

Zimmerman, J. (2014). Media bias through facial expressions on local Las Vegas television news programs: A visual content analysis [master's thesis]. University of Nevada, Las Vegas.

9 Applications to research, industry, and beyond

"It's not just what you say, but how you say it." A phrase used to describe the impact of nonverbal behavior in the communication process. For journalists whose job it is to communicate critical information to the public, nonverbal communication plays a key role. Yet, researchers have often ignored the impact of nonverbal behavior in media messaging. This book serves as a primer for those interested in continuing the exploration of this critically important element of communication, nonverbal neutrality.

This book includes a content analysis of the variability of broadcasters' nonverbal neutrality while reporting six of the deadliest school shootings in modern U.S. history. However, the implications for research and academia go well beyond these events. The chapter discusses ways in which the Nonverbal Neutrality Theory should encourage other scholars to explore nonverbal communication and nonverbal neutrality in journalism, as well as how to apply these findings in industry through individual journalists, organizations, and journalism educators.

Conceptualization of nonverbal theories

The visibility of journalists is increasing with convergent media practices; even traditional print journalists must work to produce digital and social media pieces in which they may need to be present (either visibly or vocally). Thus, convergent media practices make the study of nonverbal communication in journalism even more important.

While scholars have previously examined nonverbal communication in journalism, these studies often do not provide a true conceptualization of nonverbal communication and behaviors tied to specific nonverbal theories. This study contributes theoretically to both journalism and nonverbal scholarship by bridging the gap between these fields. This is one of the first studies to apply BECV and BET approaches to journalism studies, which helps extend those theories to a new context.

DOI: 10.4324/9781003375340-9

Nonverbal communication's role in objectivity norms

Additionally, the findings suggest neutrality can be understood and enacted not only by what journalists say, but how they say it. Those journalistic practices that encourage objectivity, such as covering the facts, sourcing through officials, framing coverage episodically, and performing the disseminator role, also predict neutral nonverbal behavior. This should encourage future scholars to study neutrality and objectivity nonverbally, not only linguistically and verbally. Objectivity and neutrality studies have often just relied on the words written or said, but these findings suggest the whole message may not be fully understood through this approach, as it leaves out a major form of information sharing – nonverbal behaviors. Thus, this work is a call for objectivity and neutrality to explore nonverbal communication patterns further and to incorporate these future findings in our conceptualizations and measurements of these key factors in journalism studies.

The findings also suggest a stronger influence of BECV-related factors on nonverbal neutrality, where broadcasters modify their nonverbal behaviors, whether consciously or not, in order to comply with the socially constructed standards of the industry. The findings suggest that even in emotional, traumatic circumstances where reaction-based factors are significant, there are other, often stronger social factors like roles, sources, and topics that continue to influence the individual level, evidence of an ongoing interplay between these levels. For journalism scholarship, BECV approaches seem more applicable since the professionalization at the social level of individual workers appears to constrain the emotional, stimuli-based reactions that BET scholars have found in general populations.

This means typifications, that previously have been studied only through linguistic standards, should begin to be reexamined with nonverbal communication practices in mind. For example, scholars could explore ways in which journalists control their nonverbal behaviors to comply with more neutral-driven roles like disseminators and the appropriate professional boundaries for journalists working in more subjective roles like adversarial and populist-mobilizer; scholars should then find the media effects on audiences for journalists using different nonverbal patterns by role. So little is known about the ways in which these typifications are practiced by journalists in terms of nonverbal communication, demonstrating a gap in the literature to be filled by future scholars.

Exploring effects of emotional leakage on air

Despite the evidence that BECV factors are stronger influences, scholars should be aware of the predictive power of individual, trauma-based stimuli. This is especially important as they apply to the normative exceptions journalists provide when deviations occur from the professional standards. Journalists I interviewed (2022) called these "gray spaces," areas where they were willing to "give a pass" to journalists showing emotions in traumatic situations; yet, exactly where those blurred boundaries exist in the profession remains murky, especially in instances outside of crisis coverage research.

Little is known about how audiences respond to these "slips" in nonverbal neutrality. Audiences sometimes empathize with the journalist, such as when meteorologist Matt Laubhan at WTVA got emotional and prayed on air as a tornado hit his community, which was received with relatively positive public response (Oliver, 2023). Sometimes they see it as ratings grabbing or insincere, such as when CNN published a video of an Indian broadcaster unaffiliated with the network breaking down on air after learning her husband was killed in a car accident she was reporting on (Jacobson, 2020). Others suggest reporting during COVID-19 gave journalists "permission to be human" as many journalists broke nonverbal neutrality on air (Jones, 2020). Further investigation of COVID's impact on nonverbal neutrality norms, as well as more understanding of audience expectations for nonverbal presentation, could help more clearly define the Nonverbal Neutrality Theory.

Scholars must also pay closer attention to the effects of vicarious trauma and continuous exposure to crisis on reporters, newsroom cultures, and production practices. While great work is being done to better understand how journalists are affected by the normalization of trauma in journalism (e.g. Belair-Gagnon et al., 2023), less is understood about the toll this vicarious traumatization and slips in work efficacy have on the products and the organization as a whole. Researchers need to call more attention to the demands on individuals, provide potential solutions for organizations, and advocate for cultural changes that protect and help journalists in crisis coverage reporting, which benefits all levels – from individual journalists, to newsroom cultures, to audiences receiving better stories and products.

Methodological applications to nonverbal neutrality

This theory also offers methodological paths for media scholars wishing to study nonverbal communication. Conceptualizing nonverbal behavior as both expressiveness and valence, the study integrates the two dominant theories of nonverbal communication, BET and BECV, in journalism nonverbal scholarship. The findings suggest these constructs are distinct, providing further evidence for nonverbal scholars who argue the distinctions of these theories.

It again points to the need for researchers to be clear in their conceptualizations and measurements of nonverbal behavior. Since the outcomes of both *NNS* and *JF* are often different and sometimes even contrary to one another within the findings of this study, it is important researchers choose the proper measurement and method to explore.

The measurement tools, *NNS* and *JF*, can also be utilized for other types of studies, including other content analysis contexts (such as natural disasters, protest coverage, traditional coverage, etc.) and other methodologies (surveys, experiments, etc.). The measurements provided useful information on the field, especially in determining exactly what types of nonverbal communication were most affected by each factor. Other scholars can utilize these variables and add others to expand current understandings of nonverbal neutrality in journalism fields.

In addition, scholars should utilize other ways of measuring the nonverbal expression of broadcasters, such as FACS or computer coding, which could help expand these findings. Future scholars can use this project to inform advancements in nonverbal theory and measurements as they apply the concepts to media.

The next steps for Nonverbal Neutrality Theory

Additionally, this study suggests ways to extend Graber's (2002) stages of crisis coverage theory, offering additional contexts through which future researchers can explore nonverbal neutrality in crisis contexts. Through Chapter 7's proposal of the Nonverbal Neutrality Theory, this work provides a theoretical basis to understand how typifications and routine coverage patterns may affect a journalists' nonverbal neutrality.

This study answered Coleman and Wu's (2006) call to explore nonverbal neutrality in non-terrorism crisis contexts, in this case school shootings, and it found notable differences. This suggests the need for further examination in future scholarship. Yet, this study is limited in its study of manmade disasters. Researchers should continue to explore the various influences in other crisis contexts, such as natural disasters, war reporting, and protest or social conflict coverage, and even non-crisis coverage to better understand nonverbal neutrality in journalism.

Additionally, adding more contexts in which to explore nonverbal neutrality's variability can only improve this theory and its applications. Scholars should explore contexts outside of traditional broadcast television news, including digital, social media, and podcasts. Given typifications and routines vary by media type, understanding the nuances for each professional field would be important to finding ways in which social expectations may shift the ways nonverbal communication is enacted by the speaker.

Variances among cultures is also important in nonverbal scholarship (Matsumoto, 2006), where nonverbal norms change vastly based on social expectations. Therefore, future scholars should focus on exploring nonverbal neutrality in different countries and journalistic systems that don't center on objectivity to see how the nonverbal neutrality norm would be enacted and understood. In their study of journalists' use of touch (haptics) in reporting after Hurricane Maria in Puerto Rico, Takahashi and colleagues (2022) noted journalists in high-contact cultures, including Arab/Islamic, Central and South American, Mediterranean, Southern and Eastern European countries, may have wider acceptance of the use of touch in reporting compared to low-contact cultures. As one of the first studies to explore nonverbal communication in other cultures and contexts, Takahashi and colleagues' study shows the importance of considering cultural differences in the application of nonverbal communication in journalism studies.

Also, this work focuses primarily on kinesics (facial expressions) and gesture nonverbal communication. Yet, there are many subdisciplines of nonverbal communication relatively unexplored, including proxemics (space), vocalics (voice characteristics), chronemics (use of time), haptics (touch), oculesics (eye movement), artifacts (clothing, objects), environment, and more. Some scholars are beginning to explore these areas. Takahashi and colleague's (2022) work explores haptics, the use of touch, for instance. In her exploration of gender in podcasting, Mottram (2017) explored vocal fry and pitch of podcasters, a form of vocalics. In an interesting combination of vocalics and proxemics, Wincott and colleagues (2021) explore the impacts of using immersive or spatialized audio forms in radio and podcast journalism. Yet, these publications are few and far between and are rarely the focus of academic training in journalism studies. Further exploration and incorporation of nonverbal communication's impact on journalism is needed.

Overall, this theory opens a door for exploring nonverbal communication in journalism, both from the perspective of content production and the ways in which audiences engage with journalists. The goal of this work is not to suggest this theory will hold in all instances of reporting, for all media types, across all cultures; in fact, in the journalism field where normative boundaries are under continuous negotiation and change, that approach would never work. Instead this work provides a foundation upon which other scholars can build and expand for a clearer picture of where those shifts in nonverbal neutrality exist and how we can assist journalists and newsrooms to cope.

Applications for the journalism field

Crisis is an everyday part of journalistic practice. Researchers suggest 81% of journalists covered at least five potentially traumatic events in just four years (Londsdale, 2022), and witnessing these crises can take a personal toll on journalists (Seely, 2019). When mentally affected through vicarious traumatization, individuals' work and routines can become less efficient and lack professional standards (Collins & Long, 2003). Yet, journalists report receiving little to no training on how to maintain normative standards of practice while undergoing crisis reporting (Deavours, 2022), nor do most organizations provide individuals who have experienced vicarious traumatization coping techniques or resources (Novak & Davidson, 2013). So how can individual journalists, their newsroom owners and leaders, and educators better prepare storytellers to maintain professional norms, such as nonverbal neutrality, for the routineness of nonroutine tragedy?

Despite working during traumatic, emotional events, broadcasters heavily rely on routine standards of practice, which have the strongest influence on their nonverbal neutrality. It could be that journalists understand expected standards of practice, including nonverbal neutrality, as a taken-for-granted professional norm and work, often unconsciously, to meet those standards in their own reporting despite what is going on around them. Most educational programs focus on the same types of typifications – roles, sourcing, framing, etc. – yet, they often do so without the context of nonverbal communication, focusing solely on linguistic critiques. This study suggests broadcasters need to be more aware of how their nonverbal communication can affect their objectivity, not relying solely on a taken-for-granted understanding of professional expectations but more clearly defining and practicing expected standards of display.

Educators and media consultants should work to train broadcasters in nonverbal management, working to control or conceal nonneutral nonverbal behaviors that would not conform to the organization's or industry's expectations of professional neutrality norms. Nonverbal communication is pervasive throughout every audiovisual report, and previous scholarship has found nonverbal neutrality variance patterns in traditional coverage as well (Zimmerman, 2014).

Thus, nonverbal neutrality must become a concept that scholars and professionals focus on in all forms of journalism. Since the behaviors of network journalists, the elite of the field, are explored here, these normative patterns likely trickle down to other forms of journalist practice to those in lower markets or positions that may model their behaviors. Closer examinations of the field's use of nonverbal behavior, discussions of appropriate and expected nonverbal displays, and trainings on these nonverbal communication areas like kinesics, gestures, and vocalics can help all journalists – from students to veterans – have more clearly defined understandings of these industry norms.

This means journalism programs, particularly those with visual storytelling foci, need to incorporate curriculum and assessments on nonverbal communication, display, and performance. While ongoing debate continues about the place of objectivity in journalism curriculum continues and educators critique professionalizing versus critical analysis approaches (e.g. Shapiro, 2015), these conversations almost always position objectivity as a solely linguistic practice. Instead, as educators continue to train journalists to be media-literate critical thinkers and facts-focused storytellers, they must also train them in the ways their nonverbal communication may affect those ideological positions.

This could be done through collaboration with nonverbal communication scholars in existing journalism classes, having journalists take nonverbal communication courses in their curriculum, or focusing assessment tools on a storyteller's presentation and nonverbal display. Some programs are even creating entire classes for visual storytellers that focus on aspects of broadcaster performance, such as the University of Alabama whose JMC 356 course "Television and Radio Performance" is described as "a practical approach to techniques necessary for effective presentation on radio, television and the internet; emphasizes copy interpretation, interview skills, and studio and field performance for microphone and camera" (UA, 2023). Courses like this, that combine theoretical knowledge of nonverbal behavior's impact on communication practices with the practical application of reporting techniques, may help journalists better understand and conceptualize how to perform nonverbally.

This training is especially important in instances that tend to be less neutral like policy discussions and first-hand accounts. These forms of journalism can be challenging to replicate in a collegiate environment, meaning the first time reporters experience these challenges is on the job; this requires the individual to learn from peers who expect them to already know how to act as some form of learning by osmosis "common sense" (Deavours, 2022). Without the proper training, individuals are left to come up with their own forms of controlling and concealing nonverbal behaviors, with varying degrees of success.

This can be corrected by having more opportunities to train and receive evaluation during simulated events, rather than real-life crises. For instance, educators or newsrooms could team up with local emergency officials during their training exercises to produce mock reports, helping reporters witness the pressures of these crises, expectations of behavior, and ways to improve their nonverbal communication in reports in a non-crisis situation. Instructors can also encourage students to go after more challenging topics in their reports, pushing them to experience tragedy and crisis while in the safety and guidance of a college classroom.

Industry and organizational crisis coverage planning

The results of this study suggest social-level factors, like role performance, sourcing, and topic, are the most influential factors on nonverbal neutrality variability. While individuals enact these typifications, journalists are working within larger social constructs of what is expected and appropriate in crisis coverage, which is often determined by newsrooms, owners, and the industry at large. Thus, as organizations create and train journalists on their crisis coverage plans, it's critical that decisions about which typifications of practice are expected include discussions of their implications for nonverbal neutrality as well.

News organizations should consider how particular patterns of work, such as roles, sources, topics, and framing, affect the overall neutrality of crisis coverage. For example, knowing those performing adversarial roles are most likely to display nonneutral nonverbal behaviors, newsrooms that are planning for and enacting adversarial journalism practices can anticipate ways in which reporters may need to adjust, mask, and/or control their typical nonverbal behaviors if they want to remain nonverbally neutral. If nonverbal neutrality issues are thought of and addressed in the planning stages of crisis coverage, especially at a managerial level, this will set clear expectations for individuals to follow on the proper nonverbal presentation.

This means newsroom leaders, owners, and the industry as a whole must have more open conversations about nonverbal neutrality, its place in the field, and how to utilize it appropriately. Currently, broadcasters are receiving no training or advice on this topic (Deavours, 2022) so they are left to figure out nonverbal expectations through social learning and individual trial and error. When nonverbal communication can have significant effects on audiences, journalists need more guidance on what is expected of them so they can work efficiently and effectively, especially during emotional and traumatic events.

Supporting individuals to prevent emotional leakage

The findings suggest typification factors at the social level have the strongest influence on nonverbal variability. This does not mean, however, that the impact of working in emotional and traumatic situations is devoid of individual effects. First, results do find significant differences in some individual-level factors, especially when considering the moderating effects of stage of coverage. Second, typifications being most influential could actually point to journalists' reliance on these routine practices as a coping mechanism, a way of compartmentalizing and focusing on efficiency and professionalism (Berkowitz, 1992). Yet these decisions are made autonomically and without evaluating their practice in the moment, and since these typifications are typically taught and discussed in terms of linguistic communication only, journalists are left without guidance for nonverbal communication. This may lead to more instances of "emotional leakage" or unintentional nonverbal behaviors (Ekman & Friesen, 1969). Focusing on protocols is also only a temporary solution and will eventually lead to a mental breakdown as the effects of trauma catch up to the individual (Collins & Long, 2003); this could mean a loss of composure nonverbally. By providing journalists with more nonverbal training, as described above, individuals may be more capable of intentional control over their nonverbal communication, and it could also help in coping with these events better as well.

Additionally, masking feelings can be damaging long-term, especially when healthy coping mechanisms aren't utilized to process the traumatic stimuli that led to masking and/or emotional leakage (Ekman & Friesen, 1969; Löfgren et al., 2016). Thus, journalists and their organizations cannot ignore the impacts of crisis on individual mental health without harming both the individual and their work. Organizations and individual journalists would be remiss in not providing healthy coping mechanisms and support for journalists.

Researchers find newsrooms often do not provide training or support for journalists to handle these traumatic situations (Deavours, 2022); others find journalists are reluctant to report trauma, discuss it within their organizations, or visit mental health professionals for fear of seeming weak (Smith et al., 2015). Research suggests journalists turn to their own forms of coping, which are usually unhealthy forms of coping such as normalizing trauma or self-medicating with alcohol or other substances (Seely, 2019). Others leave the industry due to burnout or a lack of desire to continue experiencing repeated exposure (Löfgren et al., 2016). These have long-term effects not only for the individual reporter but also for the industry and news production process as a whole.

There are many ongoing conversations in professional and academic associations around the world on the need for trauma training and resources for journalists. The Dart Center(2022) has become a critical resource for individuals, newsrooms, owners, and academics on trauma and crisis reporting, providing tip sheets, training, and more. Professional organizations like RTDNA, AEJMC, NAB, and BEA, to name a few, host panels and workshops on these topics as well. Owners are implementing new programs that support mental health and workplace happiness; the Public Media Alliance (2022) suggests more owners are feeling increased responsibility for protecting journalists' mental health in the wake of COVID-19. These kinds of programs not only protect the individuals and their mental health, but will also assist journalists in being able to control and communicate effectively through nonverbal behaviors, even during crises. Research also shows the most effective changes for employee wellbeing come from policies, making these resources an organizational intervention we all should continue to advocate for (Novak & Davidson, 2013).

Re-examining nonverbal neutrality

This research does not assume, however, that nonverbal neutrality is the best or only way of reporting during crises. Instead, it uses neutrality as the current norm of practice, widely reported as a current cornerstone of the field by broadcast professionals (Deavours, 2022). As journalists negotiate the boundaries of objectivity and neutrality, nonverbal communication must be considered.

Just as scholars suggest true objectivity is not possible to achieve (Reese, 1990), the same can be said for nonverbal neutrality – completely neutral communication is rare and often out of place in crisis contexts. Imagine a reporter reading without any emotion or urgency in their face, voice, posture, etc., as they are standing in a war-torn city; that wouldn't match the tone and seriousness of the event. Yet, journalists are without guidance on just how to know what is appropriate and when. This research suggests professional boundaries must continue to be negotiated to enable nonverbal behavior that is compassionate and human in the face of tragedy, while not crossing into perceived bias or emotional manipulation.

However, these findings suggest the opposite is happening in school shooting coverage. Broadcasters recounting the experiences of traumatized victims inside the school are more neutral nonverbally than those discussing political issues like gun control, mental health, and safety in schools. Broadcasters who are talking to victims, their families, and the communities affected are more neutral nonverbally than those talking to experts and policy influencers. This seems antithetic to the norm of objectivity that importantly informs American journalism.

Prior study suggests journalists favor a neutral approach to covering politics, even when they are covering emotional crises (Deavours, 2023). Yet, broadcasters are not doing so through their nonverbal behavior in the cases studied in this research project. This suggests the industry and academia need to consider the practical implications of this research for crisis coverage – should such coverage more closely align with their desire to be objective, particularly when addressing political aspects of crisis journalism? These types of boundary negotiation need to be researched, taught, and addressed more in academia and industry.

Conclusion: Conveying communication beyond words

This work serves as a call to journalism partners to consider the applications of nonverbal neutrality across the journalism industry and in media studies. Through its presented case study of six of the deadliest school shootings, the work hopes to give media practitioners and researchers pause when it comes to what is conveyed by nonverbal behaviors and the implications of that communication.

No journalist should have to feel like they can't be human in the midst of the crises they cover; it is neither healthy nor a long-term solution. Instead, through increased awareness and training on nonverbal communication, journalists can feel more empowered to convey information in a more conscious and purposeful way.

Because even more so than what is being said, the communication beyond words remains a critical, yet too often ignored feature of journalists' work.

References

Belair-Gagnon, V., Holton, A. E., Deuze, M., & Mellado, C. (Eds.). (2023). *Happiness in journalism*. Routledge.

Berkowitz, D. (1992). Routine newswork and the what-a-story: A case study of organizational adaptation. *Journal of Broadcasting & Electronic Media*, *36*(1), 45–61.

Coleman, R., & Wu, D. (2006, June 7). More than words alone: Incorporating broadcasters' nonverbal communication into the stages of crisis coverage theory – evidence from September 11. *Journal of Broadcasting & Electronic Media, 50*(1), 1–17.

Collins, S., & Long, A. (2003). Too tired to care? The psychological effects of working with trauma. *Journal of Psychiatric & Mental Health Nursing, 10*, 17–27.

Dart Center. (2022). Resources. Dart Center for Journalism and Trauma. https://dartcenter.org/resources

Deavours, D. (2022). Nonverbal neutrality norm: How experiencing trauma affects journalists' willingness to display emotion. *Journal of Broadcast and Electronic Media, 67*(1), 112–134.

Deavours, D. (2023). Continuing work in the face of tragedy: How broadcast journalists process vicarious traumatization through cognitive dissonance. In V. Belair-Gagnon, A. E. Holton, M. Deuze, & C. Mellado (Eds.), *Happiness in journalism* [in press]. Routledge.

Ekman, P., & Friesen, W. V. (1969). Nonverbal leakage and clues to deception. *Psychiatry, 32*(1), 88–106.

Graber, D. (2002). *Mass media and American politics* (6th ed.). CQ Press.

Jacobson, S. (2020). Crying journalists is now a clickbait genre. Columbia Journalism Review. https://www.cjr.org/analysis/crying-journalists-clickbait.php

Jones, C. (2020). 'Permission to be human': TV journalists crying on camera is understandable. Nieman Reports. https://niemanreports.org/articles/permission-to-be-human-tv-journalists-crying-on-camera-is-understandable/

Löfgren Nilsson, M., & Örnebring, H. (2016). Journalism under threat: Intimidation and harassment of Swedish journalists. *Journalism Practice, 10*, 880–890.

Londsdale, C. (2022). Taking Care: A report on mental health, well-being & trauma among Canadian media workers [pdf]. Canadian Journalism Forum on Violence and Trauma. Canadian Journalism Forum on Violence. https://www.journalismforum.ca/taking-care-report

Matsumoto, D. (2006). Culture and nonverbal behavior. In V. Manusov & M. L. Patterson (Eds.), *Handbook of nonverbal communication* (pp. 219–235). Sage.

Mottram, C. (2017). Finding a pitch that resonates: An examination of gender and vocal authority in podcasting. *Voice and Speech Review, 10*(1), 53–69.

Novak, R. J., & Davidson, S. (2013). Journalists reporting on hazardous events: Constructing protective factors within the professional role. *Traumatology, 1*, 1–10.

Oliver, D. (2023). A weatherman, a brief prayer and how journalists help during moments of tragedy, trauma. *USA Today*. https://www.usatoday.com/story/life/health-wellness/2023/03/27/mississippi-tornado-weatherman-prays-comfort-amid-trauma/11549066002/

Public Media Alliance (2022). Public media organisations providing mental health services for staff. PSM Innovations. https://www.publicmediaalliance.org/public-media-organisations-providing-mental-health-services-for-staff/

Reese, S. (1990). The news paradigm and the ideology of objectivity: A socialist at the Wall Street Journal. *Critical Studies in Mass Communication, 7*(4), 390–410.

Seely, N. (2019) Journalists and mental health: The psychological toll of covering everyday trauma. *Newspaper Research Journal, 40*(2), 239–259.

Shapiro, I. (2015). To turn or to burn: Shifting the paradigm for journalism education. In G. Allen, S. Craft, C. Waddell, & M. Young (Eds.), *Toward 2020: New directions in journalism education*. Ryerson Journalism Research Centre.

Smith, R., Newman, E., Drevo, S., & Slaughter, A. (2015). Covering trauma: Impact on journalists. Dart Center. https://dartcenter.org/content/covering-trauma-impact -on-journalists

Takahashi, B., Zhang, Q., Chaves, M., & Nieves-Pizarro, Y. (2022). Touch in disaster reporting: Television coverage before Hurricane Maria. *Journalism Studies, 23*(7), 818–839.

UA. (2023). Courses for journalism & creative media. University of Alabama. https:// catalog.ua.edu/undergraduate/communication-information-sciences/journalism -creative-media/courses/

Wincott, A., Martin, J., & Richards, I. (2021). Telling stories in soundspace: Placement, embodiment, and authority in immersive audio journalism. *Radio Journal: International Studies in Broadcast & Audio Media, 19*(2), 253–270.

Zimmerman, J. (2014). Media bias through facial expressions on local Las Vegas television news programs: A visual content analysis [master's thesis]. University of Nevada, Las Vegas.

Appendix

Content analysis coding protocol

<u>For each unit of analysis you will be given the following information already in your codebook:</u>

- Unit #
- Event (1-Columbine, 2-Virginia Tech, 3-Sandy Hook, 4-Umpqua, 5-Parkland, 6-Santa Fe)
- Event year
- Time aired (Eastern)
- Network (1-ABC; 2-CBS; 3-NBC; 4-MSNBC; 5-CNN; 6-FOX News)
- Digital link or DVD #s
- Timecode
- Hour – 1–24
- Age of victims (1-youngest (Sandy Hook/Columbine), 2-middle (Parkland/Santa Fe), 3-oldest (VT, Umpqua)
- Number of deaths, ranked (1-highest (Virginia Tech and Sandy Hook); 2-middle (Parkland and Columbine); 3-lowest (Santa Fe and Umpqua)

<u>How to code:</u>

1. For Sandy Hook, Umpqua, Parkland, and Santa Fe digital coding: open 15-minute clip based on unit #. For Columbine, Virginia Tech DVD coding: use disc.
2. Go to timecode.
3. Turn off all sound. Watch clip once.
4. Code how many **seconds** clip is.
5. Watch clip a second time with the sound off.
6. Determine nonverbal behavior for six dimensions below. **Ensure sound is off.** You may rewind or replay the unit.
    - **Eyebrows**
        - Negative if lowered or furrowed toward middle; movement is below neutral position

- Positive if raised up or not furrowed; movement is above neutral position
- Neutral if normal or expressionless; there is no movement, eyebrows are in neutral position

- **Mouth/lips**
  - Negative if corners contracted or pulled back as if in a grimace, tight, or frowning; movement is below neutral position
  - Positive if raised, or retracted and raised as if smiling laughing; movement is above neutral position
  - Neutral if normal or non-expressive; there is no movement, mouth/lips are in neutral position

- **Head**
  - Negative if head turned facing downward as if dejected or tired; head is tilted below neutral position
  - Positive if head or chin pointed up; head is tilted above neutral position
  - Neutral if normally positioned or straightforward; there is no movement, head is in neutral position

- **Face**
  - Negative if serious, intense, unhappy, or worried; facial muscles are turned downward from neutral position
  - Positive if happy, lighthearted, calm, or peaceful; facial muscles are turned upward from neutral position
  - Neutral if normal or expressionless; there is no movement, facial muscles are in neutral position

- **Body**
  - Negative if stiff or tense, the speaker is leaning forward as if hunched over; the body is below the neutral position
  - Positive if relaxed, the speaker is leaning backward as if open and inviting; the body is above the neutral position
  - Neutral if normal or expressionless; the body is straight, not leaning, and in neutral position

- **Gesture**
  - Negative if journalist engaged in a lot of gesturing, hand-waving, or so forth at shoulder level or above; hands and arms are moving below neutral position
  - Positive if small expressions with hands at waist level or below shoulder level; hands and arms are moving above neutral position
  - Neutral if none; hands and arms are not moving, they are in neutral position

IMPORTANT: Once nonverbal codes are complete for the unit, you cannot go back and change your answers.

7. **Turn sound on.** Replay unit. Mark numbers.
8. Code for journalist's **gender**.
   - 1. Female – a woman, girl; an individual of the sex typically capable of bearing young/producing eggs
   - 2. Male – a man, boy; an individual of the sex typically capable of producing small, motile gametes (such as sperm)
   - 3. Undetermined
     - *Note: on all undetermined codes, add a note in codesheet about why it couldn't be determined*

9. Code for the journalist's **race**.
   - 1. White – person of origins of Europe, the Middle East, or North Africa
   - 2. African American – person of origins in Black racial groups of Africa
   - 3. Asian – person of origins of Far East, Southeast Asia, or the Indian subcontinent
   - 4. Hispanic – person of Hispanic origin
   - 5. Native Islander – combines Native Hawaiian, Pacific Islander, American Indian, and Alaska Native definitions from U.S. Census Bureau
   - 6. Undetermined
10. Code for **affiliation**.
    - 1. Local – journalist works for local affiliate (station includes W or K at beginning). Discerned from verbal or visual cues
    - 2. National – journalist works for national affiliate like ABC News, CBS News, Fox News, NBC News, CNN, MSNBC
    - 3. Undetermined
11. Code for **location**.
    - 1. TV station/newsroom – journalists on news set, anchor desk, newsroom
    - 2. In the field, not in state – journalist not in newsroom, but not in state where event took place (examples: White House; NRA offices; etc.)
    - 3. Secondary scene – journalist is in same state of shooting but not at school or staging area (examples: community vigil, shooter's home, etc.)
    - 4. Primary scene – school or staging area of event; meet up locations for families would be included as a primary scene
    - 5. Undetermined
12. Code for the **role performance**. Pick one. If there is more than one role present, pick most prevalent.
    - 1. Dissemination – emphasizes relay of information to the public without commentary
    - 2. Interpretative – analyzes complexity of issue, addressing policies, and investigating official claims; adds commentary and interpretation

- 3. Adversarial – places media as watchdog, offering alternative viewpoints; watchdog of/for government, protecting country from outside influences
- 4. Populist-mobilizer – lets people express views, develops intellectual and cultural interests, motivates people's involvement, and points to possible solutions; works to bring community back to "normal"/status quo
- 5. Undetermined

13. Code for the **topic**. Pick only one. If more than one topic, pick most prominent.
   - 1. The events of the shooting (basic facts)
   - 2. The suspect (facts, details on his background, mental health, potential motive, etc.)
   - 3. The weapons used (including descriptions of what the weapons used were capable of and the laws for that particular weapon)
   - 4. Law enforcement and the scene (facts or statements about the ongoing investigation)
   - 5. Gun laws (not specific to the event but more broadly speaking)
   - 6. Mental health regulations (not specific to the event but more broadly speaking)
   - 7. Community coping (how the surrounding area is dealing with the tragedy; this does not include national reaction or those with weak ties to the community)
   - 8. National reactions (how the United States and international communities are responding to the event; does not include the local community or those with strong ties)
   - 9. Witness statements (those who were nearby, but not in the school at the time of the shooting; those in school at the time of the shooting are considered "survivors")
   - 10. Survivor personal stories (those who were in the school at the time of the shooting, but not those who were witnessing events outside of the school such as a neighbor)
   - 11. Details of the victims (those shot or killed during the event)
   - 12. Politician statements (includes politicians (elected or not) and advocacy groups; statements specifically about gun laws or mental health regulations should be categorized in those categories)
   - 13. School safety (generally what schools can do to keep students safe, regulations needed to increase security, or discussions of the school's current security protocols)
   - 14. Undetermined

14. Code the **frame**.

Episodic frames deal with only the event itself as a singular episode. Thematic frames deal with broader issues beyond the singular event, connecting the event to broader issues. If a story includes both frames, see which one is stronger. If there is equal representation of frames, choose 3, but do not do this unless both categories are clearly equal.

- 1. Entirely episodic
- 2. Mostly episodic with some thematic elements
- 3. Equal parts episodic and thematic
- 4. Mostly thematic with some episodic elements
- 5. Entirely thematic

15. Code for the **source**. Pick only one. If more than one source, pick most prominent source.

- 1. Elected official (a government officer who has been elected to their position such as the president, governor, mayor, etc.)
- 2. School official (an official who represents the affected school)
- 3. Law enforcement official (official who actively represents a law enforcement agency at any level (police, sheriff, FBI, etc.))
- 4. First responder (such as firefighter or medic, not law enforcement)
- 5. Legal expert (such as lawyer, political analyst, academic in politics/law)
- 6. Law enforcement expert (not currently active in law enforcement but speaks to the operations of officials, such as police/FBI analyst, former law enforcement officials, academic in fields of criminology, etc.)
- 7. Mental health expert (speaks to analysis of mental health issues including a psychiatrist, counselor, mental health advocacy group, academic in field of psychiatry, etc.)
- 8. Survivor (someone who was on the scene of the event and survived the shooting, such as a student who escaped the scene)
- 9. Witness of event (someone who was close to the event or those involved but who was not on the scene of the shooting)
- 10. Family member or friend of victim/survivor (this is someone closely related to a victim/survivor of the event such as a parent of a student or a friend of a victim who died)
- 11. Family member/acquaintance suspect (someone who is speaking about knowing the shooter(s))
- 12. Community member of current event (someone in the affected community but not directly related to a victim/survivor/shooter(s) or an elected official; an example would be a pastor who speaks to how the city is coping with the tragedy)
- 13. Survivor/victim/family of previous incident (someone who survived or is speaking about a friend/family member who died during a previous school shooting, such as a Columbine survivor, or a family member of a person who died in another shooting)
- 14. Interest group/lobby representative (a group of people seeking to influence public policy on basis of a particular common interest or concern (e.g. NRA, Coalition to Stop Gun Violence, ACLU); this does not include mental health advocacy groups)

- 15. Man-on-the-street (MOS) (someone who does not fit into any of the above categories, but is providing their personal opinion on the event, such as someone in another city talking about their fear of something similar happening in their school)
- 16. Journalist serving as first person eyewitness (this is a journalist who is discussing their personal experience while covering the crisis)
- 17. Another journalist or media outlet is cited
- 18. Unconfirmed source (the journalist specifically states that the source is anonymous, confidential, or unconfirmed; this does not apply to information shared without a source)
- 19. Undetermined
- 20. Information has no source. The information is not attributed to anyone or any institution

Researcher note – Collapse source categories by creating new variable and recoding…

- 1. Official
    - 1. Elected officials
    - 2. School officials
    - 3. Law enforcement officials
    - 4. First responders
- 2. Experts
    - 5. Legal experts
    - 6. Law enforcement experts
    - 7. Mental health experts
    - 14. Interest groups/lobbyists
- 3. Communities
    - 8. Survivor
    - 9. Witness
    - 10. Family member victims
    - 11. Family member/acquaintance suspect
    - 12. Community member of event
    - 15. MOS/national reaction
- 4. Victim of previous event – originally #13
- 5. Journalists
    - 16. First person account
    - 17. Other media sources
- 6. No source given – originally #20

16. Determine the **stage of coverage**. Based on the time of the unit (see the provided time) and the stages for the particular event (Columbine, Virginia Tech, etc.).

For all units, code "1" for stage 1, "2" for stage 2, and "3" for stage 3.

- Columbine
  - Stage 1 – April 20, 1999, 1:00 p.m.–8:59 p.m.
  - Stage 2– 9:00p.m.–April 21, 1999, 4:59 a.m.
  - Stage 3 – 5:00 a.m.–12:50 p.m.
- Virginia Tech
  - Stage 1 – April 16, 2007, 7:00 a.m.–2:59 p.m.
  - Stage 2 – 3:00 p.m.–10:59 p.m.
  - Stage 3 – 11:00 p.m.–April 17, 2007, 6:59 a.m.
- Sandy Hook
  - Stage 1 – December 14, 2012, 9:30 a.m.–5:29 p.m.
  - Stage 2 – 5:30 p.m.–December 15, 2012, 1:29 a.m.
  - Stage 3 – 1:30 a.m.–9:29 a.m.
- Umpqua
  - Stage 1 – October 1, 2015, 1:30 p.m.–9:29 p.m.
  - Stage 2 – 9:30 p.m.–October 2, 2015, 5:29 a.m.
  - Stage 3 – 5:30 a.m.–1:29 p.m.
- Parkland
  - Stage 1 – February 14, 2018, 2:00 p.m.–9:59 p.m.
  - Stage 2 – 10:00 p.m.–February 15, 2018, 5:59 a.m.
  - Stage 3 – 6:00 a.m.–1:59 p.m.
- Santa Fe
  - Stage 1 – May 18, 2018, 8:30 a.m.–4:29 p.m.
  - Stage 2 – 4:30 p.m.–12:29 a.m.
  - Stage 3 – May 19, 2018, 12:30 a.m.–8:29 a.m.

17.   Repeat all steps for the next unit, being sure to turn sound off for the nonverbal coding and turning it back on for the other categories.

Index

Page numbers in **bold** indicate tables while page numbers in *italics* indicate figures

Printed in the United States
by Baker & Taylor Publisher Services